"Few of us are totally blind or living in the dark. Our problems are much more a result of worldly distortions that lead us down destructive paths to ungodly destinations. *Reframe* is a very insightful and powerful book that clarifies the 'true' truth and how we can change our lives by changing the way we view God and our circumstances."

STEVE ARTERBURN
Bestselling author and host of New Life Radio

"This beautiful, honest, and vulnerable book has a way of stripping away your weary dogmas and legalistic lies, your fear-filled 'oughts' and 'shoulds,' and reminding you of God's amazing love and why you surrendered your life to Him. It was liberating, all over again. Read it. Weep if you must, want to, or need to. But read it."

JO SAXTON
Speaker and author, chair of 3DMovements, and co-pastor of Mission Point Church

"*Reframe* lays it out there for Christians to reconsider the assumptions they may be making about God, faith, the Bible, and themselves. It's very clear and insightful, and tailor-made for anyone who senses they are missing something significant in life . . . but can't quite place what it is. *Reframe* reveals the spaces between Christian culture and the relationship with God that we have always been promised but rarely experience."

PASTOR BRAD MATHIAS
President of Bema Media—iShine, pastor of Four Winds Anglican Mission, and author of *Road Trip to Redemption*

"*Reframe* is Brian Hardin's compelling challenge to rethink what we know about God and how we relate to Him. Too many people live with a limited, small-minded view of God—and end up living a limited life. Brian wants to change that. God has dreamed for you a bigger life, a more significant life. Hardin insists that you not settle for less and invites you to *restart* your story—and live the exhilarating, bold life God has waiting for you. If your relationship with God has turned stale and anemic, then you must read *Reframe.* Hardin says it's time to start over! Because right now, today, you can restart a completely new relationship with God."

PALMER CHINCHEN, PHD
Speaker, cultural artist, and author of *Barefoot Tribe: Take Off Your Shoes and Dare to Live the Exhilarating Life* and *True Religion: Taking Pieces of Heaven to Places of Hell on Earth*

"Brian Hardin has a way of asking the hard questions that you just can't shake. Like a modern-day mystic, his writing hits you diagonally and haunts you. In *Reframe*, Brian seeks to bring the reader to a place of spiritual awakening. I highly recommend this read to anyone who feels dead . . . as most of us do, most of the time. I wept throughout reading it, and as I did, I sensed a strange warmth arising from within."

FR. CHRIS SORENSEN
Abbot of Mission Chattanooga

REFRAME

FROM THE
GOD WE'VE MADE...

ReFRAME

TO GOD WITH US

BRIAN HARDIN

A NavPress resource published in alliance
with Tyndale House Publishers, Inc.

NavPress○®

NavPress is the publishing ministry of The Navigators, an international Christian organization and leader in personal spiritual development. NavPress is committed to helping people grow spiritually and enjoy lives of meaning and hope through personal and group resources that are biblically rooted, culturally relevant, and highly practical.

For more information, visit www.NavPress.com.

Library of Congress Cataloging-in-Publication Data

Hardin, Brian, date.
  Reframe : from the God we've made ... to God with us / Brian Hardin.
    pages cm
    ISBN 978-1-63146-447-8
  1. Spirituality—Christianity.   2. Spiritual life—Christianity.   I. Title.
  BV4501.3.H3653 2015
  248.4—dc23
                                            2015021836

Printed in the United States of America

21   20   19   18   17   16   15
7   6   5   4   3   2

For Rosalie Ann Hardin

CONTENTS

PROLOGUE

When I began to flesh out this book, I planned to write of things I thought had seasoned in my life and become a part of who I am. I wanted to transfer a few hard-won truths onto paper and offer them. Little did I know . . .

After a few months of writing, in between long stretches of a strenuous speaking schedule, I felt as if I was writing words that weren't going to connect the dots to anything. I was discouraged. Three and a half chapters into *Reframe* I threw most of it out and started over. For a writer, throwing away thousands of words and dozens of hours of work leaves a bit of a sigh and a deflated, almost nauseous feeling. But I also knew that there was more to this story. Something profound was taking shape inside me.

What I didn't know when I began to write again was that it was going to challenge my own faith to the core and force me to reframe everything I thought I knew about God.

For many, including myself for so many years, having a "relationship with God" has become synonymous with believing in God. But is this really all there is to it? I believe in a lot of people that I'm not in a relationship with and, for that matter, have never even met. I'm sure the same is true for you. It would seem that a relationship is more than just belief; unpacking what it's actually shaped like can be a bit of a mystery. It's not talked about that much—it's more assumed. But maybe it shouldn't be.

After years of poring over Scripture, I find nothing less than a God who is desperate to be with people and has done everything conceivable to enter into a collaborative and life-giving relationship with us. And so I've written this book to share my own journey, observations, and hope for a collaborative and holistic relationship with this God.

This book humbles me. It humbles me because I want it to be my life as much as I want it to be yours, and I believe everything I've written is true and available. It just requires the vigilance and commitment to accept nothing less than an all-out, all-in relationship with God. The same passion God has for us, we need to have for Him, and that has ignited a fire inside me. A revolutionary fire.

But fire burns things. It consumes things.

Much of what is being consumed are things I don't need anymore. I don't need those wounds. I don't need those idols. I don't need those ambitions. The fire is burning away things and making more room for God to occupy. But how I desperately want to hold on to some of the things that have been poison to me.

When I was nearing the end of the book, it had all but taken over my life. I couldn't sleep. The words wouldn't stop even in my dreams. I was consumed with it. I needed to know how it would end. I needed to get it out of me and release it. But the fire burns on, and I expect this is the new normal—that if I want this kind of relationship with God, it really will ruin me for anything less than all of Him. But I can tell you from a little further down the path that it's going to be worth it. This is how we were meant to live. Understanding what a relationship with God isn't, and what it could be, might just be the missing puzzle piece that completes our lives.

I'm praying for you.

— — —

One more thought. I've watched with amusement as many theological battles have been waged during the last few years—some of them pretty nasty. It's not as if this is a new thing, but I suppose the interconnected world we live in makes it more pervasive and disruptive. The truth is that anyone who steps into the public arena of faith is setting themselves up to be shot at. We've been fighting one another over the nuances of the Bible for centuries.

Via media is a Latin phrase that dates back to the ancient Greek philosophers. It means "the middle road" or "by the middle way." It found its way into church history during the Protestant Reformation, when the Church of England attempted to find its place as a bridge builder between papalist Catholics and radical reformers. I like this phrase and I've tried to write from this place—by the middle way. I didn't write anything in this book to be intentionally controversial. Maybe controversy sometimes sells books and raises profiles, but honestly, I just want to love God with all my heart and be known by Him while being true to the Scriptures. And that's what I want for you, too.

PART ONE
RETHINK

At any time, you can rethink your life and reinvent yourself.
DENISE PITRE

When we least expect it, life sets us a challenge to test our
courage and willingness to change; at such a moment,
there is no point in pretending that nothing has happened
or in saying that we are not yet ready. The challenge will not
wait. Life does not look back. A week is more than enough
time for us to decide whether or not to accept our destiny.
PAULO COELHO,
THE DEVIL AND MISS PRYM

Chapter 1

RETHINKING YOU

Wherever you go, you take yourself with you.

NEIL GAIMAN,
THE GRAVEYARD BOOK

I have seen the best of you, and the worst of you,
and I choose both.

SARAH KAY,
"AN ORIGIN STORY"

YOU

It's all about you. And it's all about what you do next.
It always has been. I know you've been told otherwise
your whole life—but it is. It has to be. Your life can be no
other way.

Does that sound somehow . . . wrong? Stay with me.

Where you've been and where you're going can only
happen with you involved. What you do with yourself
only you can decide, but make no mistake—this air in
your lungs, this next beat of your heart, the stirring in
your chest when he or she walks in the room, this life—

it's yours. Yours to unfold, unpack, screw up, crash, revive, stumble through, master, flourish, thrive in, discover. It begins with you, and if it ever ends, you'll be there. It's yours to steward and yours to give away, and no matter where you go, you are there.

Maybe God is everywhere, but being created in His *likeness* makes you *like* Him in fascinating ways. You are omnipresent to yourself.

Let that one bake in for a minute.

You are everywhere you are. God's image is embedded in you. It is as inseparable from you as you are from it. You are a constant, living reminder of who He is. You can look away but you can't get away. You can purify yourself or you can destroy yourself but you can't escape yourself. Nor can you escape God.[1] You're made this way. You're made for God.[2]

Perhaps you had no control over your creation, but you have momentous control over what you create. There's unbelievable power inside that. You matter. Really, you do. You are a creator. You fashion what becomes of the world you live in. You are finely crafted in the image of the Almighty,[3] and He is beautiful beyond description.[4] He has unquestionably created beauty within you.[5] You are His absolute masterpiece.[6]

That you are here is a gift. A beautiful, extravagant,

decadent, overgenerous, excessive gift. Something precious given by One who is hopelessly in love with you. Desperately enamored of you. Fascinated beyond words with you and longing to collaborate in what comes next for you. God is so invested in you that He put His own breath in you, molded you in His image, and stood back and said that you are "good."[7]

God was dreaming about you before you ever showed up.[8] When the attraction and rhythm and motion of your parents' union was complete, God was there providing the spark of life that has become you.[9] You're supposed to be here. It's a good thing that you are, because there's a lot riding on it.

God didn't just stop with the gift of life, though. How could He? When you've fallen in love with someone, everything, everywhere reminds you of that person. You can hardly walk down the vegetable aisle in the grocery store without wanting to buy them a ripe red tomato or a head of broccoli just to show them you can't get them off your mind. God has heaped gifts on you that are beyond extravagant.

You've been given the gift of the Holy Spirit to tell you the truth.[10] You have the gift of the Holy Scriptures to guide your every step and decision.[11] You have the gift of a gorgeous, lavish, exquisite planet to live on.[12] You've been given the gift of companionship.[13] You may have the gift of precious children.[14] You've been given the gift of an existence that will never, ever end.[15] You have the gift of God's own Son.[16] And that's barely scratching the surface of the generosity that God has bestowed on you.

Think about ears. What a gift! Without them you hear no music. No soft lullabies, no tender word from a friend's lips, no ecstasy of a lover. And what about the mountains? Oh, their beauty as the sun dips toward the horizon and engulfs the snow-capped peaks with fire, dancing and crying out worship beyond words! And think of eternity. A span of time that cannot be described by time at all. A never ending. A forever that insists and persists, promising discoveries that cannot even be imagined. A bottomless, topless, naked expanse waiting to be filled with the radiance of every experience we will ever have. And this has been placed in your heart.

Then there's love and water and green and coffee and toes and paint and sex and water lilies and chocolate and skin and dogs and motor oil and vitamin B and the smell of a newborn baby and rain and London and almonds and silk and bread and wine and the endless, endless cup of salvation. Gifts that are so extravagant and so endless that they can't possibly all be named. And they are all for you. You are beyond precious. You are beyond cared for. God has loved you well.

Maybe hearing this is like a cool sip of water when all you've been doing lately is swallowing sand. Maybe it's the other way around because you can't find any sign in your life that this could possibly be true no matter what the Bible or anyone else might say. That's okay too. No matter where you're going, you arrive by putting one foot in front of the other.

And right now, maybe one page after the other is just as important.

THE ACHE

So if all of this is true, why do you feel so empty inside? Why the struggle with anger? With depression? Why does every day feel the same? Or why does what is true feel as if it's not true at all?

There's a hunger that never quite goes away, right? An itch that doesn't quite get scratched. Life isn't working quite as it's supposed to, especially if we're supposed to be loved by God.

We think we know a lot about many things, including God. And we've created a box or a frame for this knowledge because it gives us some sort of context to explain what is unexplainable. But what if all that knowledge won't fit in the box? What if we get a bigger box and it still won't fit? What if all that we think we know has been forced into the wrong frame? We can keep looking at the picture, knowing there is something off about it, or we can take it down from the wall and reframe it.

We need to *rethink* what we know about God and how we relate to Him. Then perhaps we can *reframe* the relationship. Maybe we can give it something a little roomier. Possibly a bigger frame for our understanding of God will mean a bigger life for us. Probably if we get just a glimpse, just a taste of what's really going on, we're going to be fed up with the narrative that's been passing for our life. It won't be enough. You probably already know this. It's been the problem all along, hasn't it? You'll want to *restart* your story. A new story that feels like you. One that fits you.

And that's where we start.

GOD'S RELATIONSHIP WITH YOU

So if life is such an extravagant gift, what are you supposed to do with it? As believers, we filter this question through the lens of a relationship with God.

If I were to ask you how you know you're in a relationship with God, what would your answer be? Is it because of a prayer you spoke or portions of Scripture that you've read? Is it because you're around a lot of people who seem to be in such a relationship, or a feeling that you have inside or a theological formula you're following? Does God want to be in a relationship with you? How do you know this? Does God know who you are?

As you begin to consider these questions, slow down a bit. Ponder your answers. Be deliberate. This is very important. These questions will begin to uncover what you think you know about God and your heart's posture toward that knowledge.

"A relationship with God" or "a personal relationship with Jesus" are phrases that have become almost cliché over the years. It's shorthand for saying we are "believers." But can we be believers and not have a relationship with God? In his letter to Hebrew believers scattered throughout the Roman Empire, James said, "You say you have faith, for you believe that there is one God. Good for you! Even the demons believe this, and they tremble in terror" (James 2:19, NLT).

Most of us would say that we want a "growing relationship with God," but has this become just another of the clichés? What do we mean when we say this? Growing or deepening any other relationship involves both people. So what does that look like with God? What is it He wants from us? And how do we know for certain that we're in such a relationship? These are the things we're going to explore together. But I have to tell you, our conclusions may be different than you think. And it's going to take the fearlessness to really look at yourself.

BE HONEST

At the beginning of this story where it's all about you and the God who loves you, we have to agree to be honest. A frank conversation can bring some of the most valuable and treasured guidance for life—and we never forget it. So I'd like to have an honest discussion. No more of these conversations where we dance around what we're really trying to say.

I had a discussion recently with a man who is greatly concerned for a friend who is obese, diabetic, and consumed by and with food. The reality is that if change doesn't happen, the friend will likely die young, leaving behind people who love him and an incomplete story filled with what could have been. The man was considering how to broach the subject with his friend. It's a tough call, isn't it?

Most of the time, what we're willing to say is very subtle. We don't want to step into someone's space and create confrontation. We don't like to question individuality or freedoms. And in most cases this is healthy. At a minimum, a person who lives his or her life giving endless advice lacks the understanding of nuance. People have their own stories and reasons for the things they do. It's wise to be cautious about touching the tender parts of another person's life.

I thought a lot about my conversation with the concerned man. In that situation, it would be easy enough for him to soothe his conscience by saying, "Boy, white flour and processed sugar are really bad. They are actually the leading cause of a lot of disease." It's much harder to look someone in the eyes and say, "You're going to die if you don't change."

Don't worry. I'm not going to tell you that. But you might end up telling yourself. It's your life. It's all about you. How you live your life, how you flesh it out, is your story to tell. All the twists and turns, all the drama and intrigue and the thousands of tiny and bulky choices of each day are yours to make. You decide whether to eat the moist, creamy chocolate cake or stay focused on your fitness goals. You decide whether to drink too much and go to bed with a stranger. And when you wake up and step on the scale, you get the result of your choice one way or the other. If you yawn and roll over to find someone you don't know, well, you get the shock of your own choice.

All these little decisions become your life. You get to write the chapters with your days. You get to interact with the drama and tension that comes your way. And eventually you may come to a point where you realize you don't even like your story anymore. But what happens if you decide that with the remainder of your time, you're going to live a brand-new story? One that is not a solitary endeavor but rather a collaborative one with a God who is desperate for the opportunity to be a part of it. This new story can be a gift back to God. A page-turner that He can't put down. He gave you life, and you can give life back to Him. This is love. The give-and-take. The-send-and-receive. The back-and-forth of an alive and breathing relationship.

So this is what we need to agree on before we go any further: No one can make a change for you. It's all about you and it's all about what you do next.

Let's go on an adventure together.

Notes

1. Where can I go from your Spirit? Where can I flee from your presence? If I go up to the heavens, you are there; if I make my bed in the depths, you are there. If I rise on the wings of the dawn, if I settle on the far side of the sea, even there your hand will guide me, your right hand will hold me fast. (Psalm 139:7-10)
2. You are worthy, our Lord and God, to receive glory and honor and power, for you created all things, and by your will they were created and have their being. (Revelation 4:11)
3. Then God said, "Let us make mankind in our image, in our likeness, so that they may rule over the fish in the sea and the birds in the sky, over the livestock and all the wild animals, and over all the creatures that move along the ground." (Genesis 1:26)

4. One thing I ask from the LORD, this only do I seek: that I may dwell in the house of the LORD all the days of my life, to gaze on the beauty of the LORD and to seek him in his temple. (Psalm 27:4)

5. He has made everything beautiful in its time. He has also set eternity in the human heart; yet no one can fathom what God has done from beginning to end. (Ecclesiastes 3:11)

6. For we are God's masterpiece. He has created us anew in Christ Jesus, so we can do the good things he planned for us long ago. (Ephesians 2:10, NLT)

7. God saw all that he had made, and it was very good. (Genesis 1:31)

8. Before I formed you in the womb I knew you, before you were born I set you apart. (Jeremiah 1:5)

9. For you created my inmost being; you knit me together in my mother's womb. (Psalm 139:13)

10. But when he, the Spirit of truth, comes, he will guide you into all the truth. He will not speak on his own; he will speak only what he hears, and he will tell you what is yet to come. (John 16:13)

11. Your word is a lamp for my feet, a light on my path. (Psalm 119:105)

12. God blessed them and said to them, "Be fruitful and increase in number; fill the earth and subdue it. Rule over the fish in the sea and the birds in the sky and over every living creature that moves on the ground." (Genesis 1:28)

13. Two are better than one, because they have a good return for their labor: If either of them falls down, one can help the other up. But pity anyone who falls and has no one to help them up. Also, if two lie down together, they will keep warm. But how can one keep warm alone? Though one may be overpowered, two can defend themselves. A cord of three strands is not quickly broken. (Ecclesiastes 4:9-12)

14. Children are a heritage from the LORD, offspring a reward from him. (Psalm 127:3)

15. For the wages of sin is death, but the gift of God is eternal life in Christ Jesus our Lord. (Romans 6:23)

16. For God so loved the world that he gave his one and only Son, that whoever believes in him shall not perish but have eternal life. (John 3:16)

Chapter 2

RETHINKING
THE BOX

Theology is rather a divine life than a divine knowledge.

JEREMY TAYLOR, "SERMON VI,"
THE WHOLE SERMONS OF JEREMY TAYLOR

The devil is a better theologian than any of us and is a devil still.

A. W. TOZER

*It is not objective proof of God's existence that we want but the
experience of God's presence. That is the miracle we are really after,
and that is also, I think, the miracle that we really get.*

FREDERICK BUECHNER,
THE MAGNIFICENT DEFEAT

RUINED

I craned my neck back so that I could see the top of it.
After all the years of dreaming I finally stood at the base of
St. Martin's Cross on the remote Scottish island of Iona. I
stared into the weathered Celtic knots carved twelve centuries earlier and drank in the serenity of the abbey. It
caught my breath.

Getting to the island felt more like a pilgrimage than
anything else. I'd wanted to make this journey for most of

my adult life. The way the abbey was founded has always inspired me—St. Columba stepping into a tiny boat and setting sail with no destination in mind other than to be carried by providence to wherever God would take him, even if that meant to the bottom of the sea. It's a picture of a man ruined for anything but a moment-by-moment relationship with God. It's a profound image of trust and collaboration in what comes next. There's a wildness about it that awakens something deep inside me. I've made no plans to put the car in cruise control out on the highway and climb into the backseat just to see where I end up, but sometimes I can feel the echoes of what it might be like to be ruined for anything but a genuine collaboration and deep friendship with God, and I want it. But is it even possible to live from that place?

I was driving home from the city a couple of months ago, and for some reason I started speaking out loud to God. I wasn't asking Him for anything. I wasn't verbally processing anything with Him. I was just talking. Quickly I realized that the words falling from my lips were more of a confession than a conversation. I was speaking things that had been haunting me for years: "I'm too far into this with You to get out now. This *has* to be real. You *have* to be there. But I don't want to find out I've got it all wrong about You. I don't want to waste my life chasing after something honestly but in the end be completely wrong. I don't want to pursue You while believing an honest lie."

The words tumbling from my lips were the sincere restlessness coming from my heart. I went with it. I followed the trail as it looped its way through my childhood assumptions and adult conclusions, over the peaceful vistas and into the dark valleys of my life. Over the course of several hours, then several months, I began to understand the places I'd been completely building a platform of faith and then boxing it up in ways that were keeping me from the intimacy with God I craved.

COMPOSITE GOD

There is a fascinating story in the first book of Chronicles about the ancient warrior King David. After dramatically conquering the city of Jebus and beginning the process of converting it to the City of David, he constructed a magnificent palace for himself. It was the first royal residence for any king of Israel, and the Hebrews finally had something they could look to with pride and a sense of identity. David truly loved God. He was a passionate king who devoted himself fully to whatever he set his heart on—his people, his women, his battles, or his God.

Once the palace was complete, David realized that God

had no place to live that was nearly as nice. For two centuries God had been completely renovating the Jewish identity from that of Egyptian slaves to God's chosen people, and during this process they'd been meeting Him in a tent that traveled with them. David began to feel guilty that he lived in a cedar palace while the Lord lived in a tent, so he had a conversation with the prophet Nathan about it. Nathan told him to follow his heart and build God a magnificent dwelling place—but immediately following the conversation, God came to the prophet and instructed him to return to David at once with a message.

> You are not the one to build a house for me to live
> in. I have never lived in a house, from the day I
> brought the Israelites out of Egypt until this very
> day. My home has always been a tent, moving from
> one place to another in a Tabernacle. Yet no matter
> where I have gone with the Israelites, I have never
> once complained to Israel's leaders, the shepherds of
> my people. I have never asked them, "Why haven't
> you built me a beautiful cedar house?"
>
> I CHRONICLES 17:4-6, NLT

It wasn't until after King David's death that his son Solomon was allowed to build the temple of God. This was long after the new capital city had become the heart of Jewish culture—and long after God had continued to establish His presence out among His people, not in a box allocated for Him to dwell in.

For thousands of years we've been building a box for God, a composite of who we think He is. We've added to it and subtracted from it over the centuries. Different tribes of believers consider certain characteristics or personality traits of God more true to who He really is, and thus more important than other traits. Some people focus on God's righteous judgment while others spend their time searching for the movements of the Holy Spirit. Some feel that what is most important about God is His love or justice, while still others just want to know the future and where we are on the continuum. It's endless. When these varied convictions start rubbing against one another, though, we struggle and wrestle with each other to be right while adding more fragments to the composite.

Over time we've compiled an enormous amount of data about God. We know more now about who we think He is and what we believe He does and does not do than at any other point in history. It's as if we've created a collective 3-D model of sorts, and this is who we believe God is. But trying to pull together all these facts and data about the unfathomable, sovereign God is like trying to put wind in a box. If the data, facts, and formulas are all we have to hold on to as a relationship with God, then we simply have placed in a box what the wind has blown in. But we do not have the wind. We're just enclosed in a box of our own construction. And God will not live in our box. He's not even interested in it.

GETTING OUT OF THE BOX

When I began to discover this box I'd built for a composite God, my first stop to get out of it was at one of the many dusty copies of the Scriptures that I had lying around the house. It became the only stop I needed. I thought I had an understanding of the Scriptures. I also thought they were irrelevant to modern life other than to bring hope for something better in a far-off place called eternity.

I reasoned that if the Bible was the words God wanted to tell people, then I needed to read every word He had to say and let Him speak for Himself for once. What I found in that Bible were many stories of people just like me. Sure, they were living in another time and had a different culture and different customs, but they were after the same thing I was in life. And God was there with them in all of it.

I discovered that God wasn't nearly as angry as the composite had made Him out to be. He had been hijacked somewhere along the way. He wasn't a sadistic tyrant but rather a jilted lover—a desperate creator doing everything conceivable to protect what He loved and to restore what He was given permission to touch. And that was before I even got to the New Testament. When I read the Gospels cover-to-cover for the first time, I fell in love. Discovering that God would come to earth and live in the filth of this place—that He not only understood humanity but was willing to be in all of the drama of life together with me— changed the entire paradigm. It felt as if a tender caress was brushing away the grime of all the struggle it took to live. It felt like love. It felt like home.

I had a frame I once held God in. But it was wrong. And when I let God speak for Himself, I found that He wanted to—He actually did want a relationship with me. And He does want a relationship with you. So why do we insist on having the box?

CRITERIA

Often we approach our relationship with God using different criteria than we would any other relationship in our lives. We're created to be relational beings, but relating to God feels somehow different. There seem to be more rules, and some of them we don't fully understand. We believe He loves us unconditionally, but we're often left wondering where we stand with Him. The relationship feels like it's predicated on special conditions, like we need to make sure we read all of the fine print. But is this how it works? Does this relationship have a variable interest rate that adjusts itself based on our performance? If we go to bed having blown the whole day, do we wake up with different terms in the relationship?

A relationship that looks more like a contractual agreement than a life-giving collaboration is no relationship at all. It certainly isn't enough to perpetuate the relationship or a place God would want to live. Jesus spoke of this in a confrontation with Jewish religious leaders found in John's Gospel:

> You study the Scriptures diligently because you
> think that in them you have eternal life. These
> are the very Scriptures that testify about me,
> yet you refuse to come to me to have life.
>
> JOHN 5:39-40

The religious leaders, in an attempt to protect their traditions and faith in the Mosaic law, were blinded to the fact that God Himself was standing right in front of them. They were so entrenched in getting their belief system correct so that God would relate to them, they missed the fact that God was right there relating to them in person.

So maybe it's not God who has made this so complicated. Maybe we've turned Him into something He's not.

AS HE IS

We believe that God exists. We also believe in certain characteristics that make Him who He is. You probably believe that God loves you and wants a relationship of some sort with you. Most of us think that He has a set of rules and ethics we need to follow to be in His good graces and that following these leads us into a relationship. We'd probably say that, because God wants some sort of relationship with us, we should likewise want a relationship with Him.

But who is this God with whom we're in a relationship? When you think of your relationship with God, whom are you talking about? Some of us focus on the person of Jesus. Others would say that the Holy Spirit's presence in our lives is what guides us, while still others see the Almighty Father. Some find their sense of God in church history or from the Scriptures or from our faith community or the Internet or any number of spokespersons. But is it possible to discover God for ourselves in a personal way, or has God invited us into a relationship and then cloaked Himself so that we can't understand and know Him no matter how we try?

Maybe we've tried to create God in our own image and then attempted to force Him to be who we want or need Him to be. But life-giving, collaborative relationships only work when two people have permission to be who they are. One of the beautiful things we find in the gospel of Jesus is that we are allowed to come as we are into the relationship. Do we reciprocate this? Are we allowing God to come as He is? Or do we continue to force Him into little theological boxes?

THEOLOGY DOESN'T EQUAL RELATIONSHIP

In this age of reason, all the data and facts about God can become nothing more than a golden calf—an idol that we call God and bow down in worship to. What God desires is that we love *Him* with all our heart and soul and strength because this is precisely how He loves us back (Deuteronomy 6:5; Matthew 22:37; Mark 12:30-31; Luke 10:27).

Far too often we are misled into believing that the more data and facts we can accumulate about God, the closer we are to Him. We exchange knowledge *about* Him for a relationship *with* Him. The great irony about this is that we don't treat any other relationship this way. We wouldn't be able to because it's not a relationship at all.

Imagine taking your spouse to a nice dinner on St. Valentine's Day and staring into her eyes. You tell her that you are desperately in love and so grateful to have her in your life because you've been studying the data and facts about her and these have left you breathless with passion. This would not likely bring the romantic end to the evening you might have hoped for.

Why do we suppose this would work with God? Knowledge about someone isn't a relationship with them, and our theology or doctrine cannot save us when our world falls apart any more than our nicely built houses can save us in an F5 mega-tornado.

If, before I met my wife, Jill, I had mysteriously received several large boxes filled with a library of photos, personality profiles, stories, and videos all meticulously outlining who she would be, I might have found that to be a treasure. I could pore over every page, watch the videos, and stare at her in high resolution. The more time I spent with the data, the more I could begin to feel as if I knew everything about her. But even if the documentation were unspeakably thorough, knowing almost everything about her would not be the same as knowing her.

Were this analogy to play out and I suffered hardship

and loss, you wouldn't find me in the attic surrounded by the paperwork and DVDs. It would not be the documentation of who my wife is that would bring me comfort. It would be her. There is no replacing her presence. Every day is a new chapter and adventure in getting to know her. This is what relationships are shaped like. I can't just get everything down pat and expect her to stay put so that I can have the perfect "theology" of my wife, creating my doctrine of who she is and putting our lives in a tidy little box. Life doesn't work that way, and neither does God.

I'm not saying that theology isn't important. It's extraordinarily important because it provides a framework. It grants us access to thousands of years and millions of lives of men and women who have devoted themselves to sharing their experiences with God. Completely dismantling this framework would be like trying to live in a home without studs. The whole thing would fall down. Doctrine formulated from theology is also very important. It becomes the drywall and flooring, the paint and doorframes of our faith. We need this. But more than all of this we need God. Without God none of it matters. A nice house with no one in it is nothing but a box full of possibilities. It's the love and struggle and beauty and commitment and promise of the people inside the house that make it a home, just as it's the commitment and intertwining of lives that make a relationship real.

Spending our lives trying to find the box, control the box, and then defend the box will prove futile. And trying to call the box our relationship with God will prove dramatically unfulfilling because it's attempting to be in a relationship with data and not a living being.

God will not dwell within the human constructs of our theology. His being and existence will not reside only within our information about Him. Our theology will never be able to fully explain Him or replace a life-giving connection to Him. It's not possible. Even God Himself seems to have difficulty explaining who He is in human terms. The most profound description He offers is, "I AM WHO I AM" (Exodus 3:14).

So even with the framework of theology, we're left searching for the perfect understanding. Theology and doctrine can't flesh God out completely. After all this time, our composite still has gaps.

GAPS

People generally don't do well with gaps. We don't live very well in the tension of mystery. There have been times in history when we were more at ease with it, but not these days. Reason and logical proof of something are our main criteria for acceptance. If we can't explain something, we either dismiss it or assume we'll eventually figure it out with logic. And still we have gaps.

The love gap, for example, remains a great mystery. We understand biology and the consuming need for our species to survive. We have psychological models that explain the hormonal changes in our brains when love and attraction are present, but we cannot fully understand why a person would set aside all their self-preservation instincts and lay their life down for someone else. This mystery falls somewhere in the realm of God's embedded image in us, and we cannot decrypt it.

We can explain the physiology and psychology of sex, but we can't explain the way two souls are united as one. We can't truly articulate how lovemaking is a physical expression of a much deeper union that far surpasses the intertwining of bodies. We can't explain love, but life loses most of its meaning and drive without it.

In order to fill the gaps in routine daily life, we'll typically jump to a conclusion or make an assumption because we prefer a seamless, plausible explanation that our minds can rationalize as true. In doing this we gain the illusion of stability. Anything else leaves us uncertain, and we want certainty more than we want mystery.

Filling the Gaps

Assumptions often do more than just lead us to unfair opinions. They invite us to fill in the gaps with guesses. Once the gaps are plausibly filled, we begin to believe the guess as fact—even when it may be completely wrong. This happens all the time.

Let's say you had a conversation with an employee several months ago, and she confided that things haven't been going so well in her marriage. You gave her words of encouragement and a comforting hug, and that was the end of it. A week ago you noticed her alone during her lunch break, her head in her hands. Later that same day one of her coworkers stepped into your office and told you that she had been unusually short with him about a project they were working on together. The assumption? Things have gotten worse in her marriage. Maybe even to the breaking point, based on her current behavior.

That evening over dinner you tell your spouse you think one of your employees is about to get a divorce and you need to figure out how to manage the fallout in the office and spread the workload. Do you know this? Absolutely not. You haven't heard a word from her. The truth could be anything. It could be as simple as her young child is sick and kept her up all night. Her marriage is doing great but she's exhausted today. But because of the assumption, a false reality has been created.

The Battle for the Gaps

If we start talking about the gaps in our faith or the mystery that surrounds what we believe, we get *very* nervous. We accept that the God we have a relationship with is vastly beyond our comprehension and that there are things we don't understand because, frankly, we have no choice. It will one day all be revealed, we believe, and typically we think this will happen as soon as we die. This perspective gives us a point to defer the unexplainable to, a compartment in which to put all that we can't know for certain. We prefer to focus on what we *can* know.

What we believe we *can* know, as I mentioned earlier, is all the collected data and theological formulas that have been crafted around the mystery over the centuries—our God model. We've created complex theological dogmas about nearly everything spiritual. It's the framework or structure of our faith, and we need it. From this framework we build our doctrines, ethics, and creeds or statements of faith. This standardized common understanding helps us arrive at our accepted explanations for everything from salvation to the nature of God and the purpose of man.

But gaps still remain—plenty of them. Inside these

gaps and nuances are widely varied ways of looking at things, and we've wrestled with them and at times against each other, throwing all the weight of Scripture behind what we've been trying to prove for centuries. Skirmish lines have been laid that we feel we must defend. We'll struggle against one another over the nuances as if our entire faith depends on it—even if that means we have to leap to conclusions or make a guess to fill in the gaps. We believe we are defending God and our relationship with Him. But is this what a relationship looks like? Is this how a first-person, collaborative relationship works? When we argue as fact what we certainly cannot know, we run the risk of creating a spiritual reality that isn't real at all. And there are plenty of things we cannot know.

Don't believe me?

Consider for a moment: Can you sin after you die? You can formulate whatever dogma you wish, but none of us can know the answer to this question firsthand. If we can't sin after we die, then the whole notion of a relationship based on free will and love vanishes. Is that what happens? And if it doesn't, then the possibility of sin must reach beyond the grave. Possibly we can't fathom how we'd want to sin after being in the presence of God, but that didn't seem to work for Adam and Eve. And if we can sin, what happens if we slip up? Do we go straight to hell then?

Our accepted orthodox theology guides our understanding about eternal separation from God if we die in sin without Jesus, but we don't really have much of a formula for what might occur if we sin after we've left our bodies. Satan was cast down for trying to exalt himself above God, but that was before Jesus came to earth. Will God's mercy and the sacrifice of Jesus cover us if it's just a nanosecond of pride that we self-correct after we die? Or is that grace just for flesh-dwelling humans?

This isn't meant to be an exercise in unnerving theoretical theology. It's just a tiny discussion of one little gap. And no matter how forcefully we want to fill in the gaps, we most assuredly do not know everything, and we probably know far less than we think we do. Even if we did know everything, it isn't the same as being in a relationship *with* God.

When we dig in deep with all our facts, assumptions, and data, we quickly become trapped. Unchecked, this eventually breeds a subtle superiority complex within us. We start believing that what we've defended and accepted as absolute truth is the only true way to look at an issue. Within this view, those who believe differently are either outside the boundaries altogether or sadly deceived and missing out on all God has for them. All of a sudden we find ourselves acting as if we're sovereign and our judgments are eternal. And just like that, we're back at the forbidden tree again with all our knowledge of good and evil, choosing to be our own god. But these theological skirmish lines are not as unshakable as we might think. The intricacies all break down to a core at some point.

AT THE CORE

Imagine that a person confesses with their mouth Jesus as their Savior and believes with all their heart that God raised Him from the dead. They believe He is the Son of the living God who died to take their sins away, and they accept the offer of this undeserved grace. We'd probably agree that this person has become a follower of Christ as traditionally outlined, with the full hope of eternal life with God.

As purehearted as they might be, if they inadvertently also wind up believing some things that are not accurate about their faith or about God, will these errors upend the whole thing? Put another way, what does a person have to also believe—if they truly believe in Jesus—that will ruin everything? The answer, of course, is that we probably all believe things that, in the end, are not completely accurate, but if we are believers this cannot destroy the bonds of love and the relationship we have with God.

My sons and my daughter may indeed believe things about me that are incorrect or nuanced according to the way they know me as their father. They certainly have a different understanding of me than I do of myself, but none of this makes them any less my children. If they spend their whole lives simply trying to figure me out by talking to one another about me, they will know far less truth about me than if they crawl into my lap or sit on the couch and talk to me. And believing the right things about me isn't the same as knowing me. Either way, they are still my children, and nothing they believe about me, right or wrong, will change that.

All of our theological formulas break down to a much simpler core if we face them honestly. And we find that many of the things we spend our time trying to cement into place are not only debatable but also nonessential. Perhaps they are worthy of consideration, but it's unlikely they are worth going to battle over. If these things were crystal clear, there wouldn't be room for debate. God has made clear what He has chosen to reveal. Other things, perhaps, He's waiting to reveal within the intimacy of an actual relationship.

If Jesus had wanted to solidify every single Christian doctrine and lock into place every conceivable eventuality, then He could have simply sat down with a scribe and dictated the New Testament from His own lips before departing. Instead God chose to continue to speak as He always has—by inspiring His people.

As vastly superior as God is to us and as little of Him as we might be able to grasp with human understanding, He has always condescended that we might know Him. He's always revealing Himself to us. He is very present to those who are ruined for anything else but knowing Him (Psalm 25:14).

So getting to know God is really not as mysterious and complicated as we've made it. As beings created in His image, we already have relationship built into our spiritual DNA. It's like every relationship we've ever begun. We begin with an honest conversation. As a relationship progresses, we become more honest and reveal more and more of who we are. Over time we feel safe and comfortable, and trust is given. Eventually we become aware that we've fallen in love, and this leads us deeper in our level of intimacy. Eventually we commit everything we are to the one we love. Fully given to the relationship, we can be completely naked, unashamed, and unafraid.

This is far more true to what God is looking for when He invites us to love Him with all our hearts—that we might be naked and unashamed in the relationship. We are wired to know Him. This whole lavish world was created as a gift to us, and it continually reminds us of Him in every conceivable way. We are made in His image. We're connected to Him in our DNA. His breath of life is in us. Why would we settle for data or formulas when we can have the real thing?

A relationship with God cannot be the lifelong attempt to simply get our beliefs correct. This is not the goal of any relationship. The goal is that we are with each other, that we are for each other, and that we love each other unconditionally. This is what God has offered to us. Are we investing the same back into the relationship? Or have we been exchanging the offer of a life-giving, collaborative relationship *with* Him for the rigid attempt to believe all the right things *about* Him?

We urgently need to reframe our relationship with God. It is not theology or doctrine or dogma or facts or data that has saved us. It is God who has rescued us. Even the most perfect theology does not have the power to save us. No amount of "quiet time" devoted to studying facts about God can replace inviting Him into every thought, word, and deed of our lives. Facts and theories can only point us toward something. Without a firsthand, first-person relationship with the Almighty, we have nothing but gigabytes of data.

I want to be ruined for anything less than a life-giving connection to God. Don't you? If we ever hope to get to this place, we have to be willing to acknowledge that what we think we know is not all there is—and that God knows everything and wants to share it in a collaborative relationship with us. We also have to acknowledge that believing the right things about God is not the same as being in a relationship with Him. I'm not suggesting that we destroy the model. I'm saying there is more. So much more that God would reveal of Himself if we'd stop confining Him in our lives to what we can control and manage.

May we be strong enough to be weak enough to let God be who He is inside us. May we pursue Him with all our hearts and minds and strength, and may what we find in letting go of what we think we know be a deepening intimacy with Him. May we be ruined for anything but this, and may our lives echo what the warrior-poet David penned long ago.

O God, you are my God;
    I earnestly search for you.
My soul thirsts for you;
    my whole body longs for you
in this parched and weary land
    where there is no water.
I have seen you in your sanctuary
    and gazed upon your power and glory.

Your unfailing love is better than life itself;
    how I praise you!
I will praise you as long as I live,
    lifting up my hands to you in prayer.
You satisfy me more than the richest feast.
    I will praise you with songs of joy.

I lie awake thinking of you,
    meditating on you through the night.
Because you are my helper,
    I sing for joy in the shadow of your wings.
I cling to you;
    your strong right hand holds me securely.

PSALM 63:1-8, NLT

Chapter 3

RETHINKING GOD

*Misunderstanding is one of the worst of ill
feelings which can spoil many lives.*

LAKSHMI MENON

*"Most of the trouble in life comes from
misunderstanding, I think," said Anne.*

L. M. MONTGOMERY,
ANNE OF THE ISLAND

A CHILDISH MISTAKE

I was nine when it happened. Boys are prone to rough-housing and mischief. It was like any other day—monkey bars, kickball, and tag. We loved to play tag. On the fourth-grade playground of the tiny Lutheran school I was attending, a boy came flying by me at top speed, trying to outrun another boy who was closing in. My heel happened to be in his path, and he went airborne.

For a moment it was a thing of beauty, but gravity pulled him back to earth face-first onto the ground. For one small beat everything was calm, and then his scream filled the air. There was blood. Teachers came running. The next thing I knew, the boy's arm was extended in my direction, a shaking finger pointing directly at me. He tearfully claimed that I had stuck my foot out to purposely trip him, and he demanded justice.

A large hand grabbed the back of my neck, squeezing me tightly, as I was marched back into the school. I protested my innocence, so shocked at the accusation that I almost couldn't believe what was happening. Eventually I was deposited into an unused storage room and left alone. I sat at a rickety broken desk, feeling certain the adults would sort out the truth. As much mischief as I'd stirred up in my life, this was one time when I'd done absolutely nothing wrong. I was just there at the wrong place and time. I hadn't even seen him coming.

The door creaked open. The principal entered, his face a study in controlled anger. His terse words matched the look on his face as he demanded my confession. I began to cry. I described how I'd been playing tag with some of the other children and hadn't even seen this boy running toward me. I had not intentionally tripped him. I had no reason to make him fall.

The principal looked me straight in the eyes and said, "You're lying."

He produced a long, blue board. I hadn't noticed it when he entered the room.

"You're getting two for tripping him and two for lying to me," he announced.

My jaw dropped in disbelief. "But I didn't do anything," I pleaded.

The man wasn't moved. "Bend over and grab the edge of that desk" were his final instructions.

And I had no choice.

I had done *nothing* wrong. And that knowledge hurt worse than the *whap, whap, whap, whap* that followed. Swats at school were the worst possible humiliation for a student. And I'd done nothing to deserve them. Nothing at all.

After I dried my tears, I returned to my classroom, where my desk had been moved into a corner. Humiliated in front of my classmates, I sat there, isolated, for the rest of the day.

The whole thing was a misunderstanding. None of it was true. None of it was fair. And it was the first time in my life that I'd seen grown-ups make a colossal mistake. Beyond my humiliation was fear. Justice had not been served. What had been done was not right. That day taught me that I was at the mercy of people who could let me down.

MISUNDERSTOOD

I've been let down many times since then. Some have cost me dearly. But what about when we feel as if it's God who has let us down? I know. Even after all this talk about how much He loves us, and the beauty of being ruined for everything but a vibrant relationship with Him, there's no point in pretending we're not confused about His role in our lives sometimes. It's a startling contrast. Why can He seem so present one day and lost in a gray mist that no prayer can seem to penetrate the next? And in fairness, there has to be someone to blame for the confusion we face. We don't usually start with God, but if we can't find an answer we often end up there. God has become the cosmic trash heap for all humankind's unexplainable suffering. He's apparently got His hands in everything from tornadoes to human trafficking. From cancer to the reason the car wouldn't start this morning. And this is the God we're supposed to be in a relationship with?

Or is it?

So many times I've cried out to God about a struggle or hardship I was facing. As I poured out the situation, begging for intervention, I dragged unspoken suspicion along with me without even knowing it. "Why did You do this to me?" That would have been a more honest and true way to speak my heart. "Why did You let this happen to me?" But this isn't a prayer we openly say or even acknowledge very often. It feels guilty and shadowy and overflowing with dark things that can't be taken back if we voice them.

Perhaps much of this confusion arises from a very distorted view of the relationship. God does have a role to play in our lives, but we also have a role to play in His. Think about that for a moment. You have a role to play in God's life. Relationships at their core are always collaborative, and good relationships are the ones that are life giving to all involved. They're not one-sided. And misjudging someone over and over is a terribly one-sided relationship.

The delicate agreements and assumptions we make in these moments cling to us like burrs because at times it feels as if He's just not paying attention. They estrange us from the relationship because we have expectations that aren't being met. How often do we consider that our own choices, and not God's leading, may have led to the circumstances we are facing? Do we ever consider that the situation also has an effect on God? We look for God to get us out of trouble and wonder why He allows us to get into it in the first place without owning our own actions—a complete misjudgment.

We've all probably been misjudged at one point or another. It's a terrible feeling, isn't it? Especially when there is no way to set the record straight. We feel sentenced unjustly for a crime we didn't commit. Our character is marked with a black smudge that may possibly fade with time but feels like it will never really go away. But maybe we do the same thing to God. Maybe He isn't the one to blame for much of what He's accused of. Maybe He's been just as misjudged and misunderstood as we have.

So why do we leap to these assumptions?

HEARSAY

You've probably heard a lot of things about God. I have. Heaps of explanations are available about what God will and will not do. I've listened to loads of anecdotes about how He works, and certainly millions of words have been written to unveil His true nature and character. People have even told me what they think His favorite music is and what sorts of sins He hates most.

This endless stream of information about the way God works led me to believe that if I could just get the recipe right, find the correct formula, and follow all the steps in sequence, then I could get Him to move on my behalf and show me some of His amazing love. Usually this meant that He would do whatever I was asking. I thought that if my life were in proper order and I were following the prescription, I could get what I wanted or needed. And it was frustrating when that didn't work. I was following the program, and it felt like He just wasn't coming through. Like we talked about in the last chapter, I'd framed a complete picture of a God I thought I knew, and it was mostly based on things I'd heard *about* Him rather than on things I'd actually experienced in a relationship *with* Him. I'd bought into the composite God. But if we're going to make declarative statements or even have quiet assumptions about someone, the fair thing would be to get to know them well enough to personally form those opinions.

In a court of law you can't testify to the character of a person based on things you heard other people say. That's called hearsay. You can only testify to the things you know firsthand. Through some really intimate soul-searching I began to realize I'd formulated much of my relationship with God based on hearsay—what I'd heard other people say about Him—which resulted in some massive assumptions and misgivings.

Job said, "I had only heard about you before, but now I have seen you with my own eyes. I take back everything I said, and I sit in dust and ashes to show my repentance" (Job 42:5-6, NLT). How much of your relationship with God is based on your firsthand knowledge of Him? What do you actually know of God for yourself because of your intimacy with Him? What cherished memories and experiences do you have that only you and He share? These are questions worth spending some time on.

I thought I had an understanding of God, but I'd never considered much of what He had to say for Himself. I'd never read the Bible in context. I'd never framed a relationship with Him based on personal interaction with the heart of the stories found in Scripture or on time spent getting to know Him without a personal agenda. I thought my relationship with God was growing based on the volume of study I could do about Him. I thought that the more I could know about Him, the closer I would be to Him. I knew plenty of Bible verses, but taking verses out of context and using them as proof of God's character is like reading a couple of lines of the president's State of the Union Address and claiming that you know the president personally and understand his complex vision for the nation.

This kind of thinking is heavily influenced by our culture. For example, we turn celebrities' lives into products we consume. We say things like, "You're an idiot if you like his music," implying that *he* is an idiot and makes substandard art for the weak of intellect. Or we say, "She's such a total tramp," as if we know the inner workings of her heart and have watched her life derail while pleading with her to change course. Our conclusions about them are based mostly on hearsay and assumption.

This isn't reserved just for celebrities. We do the same to each other. We can turn people's lives into something we consume as a dark form of amusement. We measure ourselves against others and derive an odd sort of identity through doing so. But there is always more to a person's story. If I were to, for example, hear from a former classmate the naked details of that one crazy year you had in college and make those stories the judge and jury on your character and future, I'd be completely misjudging who you are now and who you're becoming.

This isn't a new phenomenon, unfortunately. Throughout the Scriptures and all of human history, we see our constant willingness to make broad and unfair assumptions about people and then live as if the assumptions were true. It was this very mentality that had throngs of people laying down palm branches and shouting, "Hosanna," for Jesus in first-century Jerusalem, only to turn on Him and nearly riot in their bloodlust for His crucifixion a few days later.

We're a fickle people when we assume too much and devour all the gossip and hearsay we can and then live as if it were all fact. And we can be just as fickle when it comes to God. It leaves us with a very fractured and shallow understanding of what a relationship with Him could be and taints the other relationships in our life.

WHERE IT STARTS

Where do all our misunderstandings and misgivings about God come from? Genesis 3 records one of the most tragic events in human history—the fall of humanity and the end of innocence. Adam and Eve are in the Garden of Eden, created as perfect beings. She has a perfect body that would make any man do a double-take and make any woman redden with jealousy. Adam is no slouch either. He's perfect too—perfect hair, perfect physique, and perfect teeth. But there is so much more to these creatures than their physicality or sexuality. They are perfect. Period. They're healthy, smart, and sinless. God has created them in His own perfect image, and He is so proud of them that He comes to walk with them in the cool of the evening.

There are two trees in this beautiful garden. One offers life, and the other God forbade them to eat from—the tree of the knowledge of good and evil.

Adam and Eve enjoy perfection and a deep, conversational intimacy with God. They have eternal life and all the beauty of God's perfect creation crafted just for them. They have everything anyone could ever hope for. They have no knowledge of sin or death or evil. They probably would have needed faith to believe those things even existed because they'd never experienced them.

And then a tragic conversation takes place between the woman and a serpent hanging from the branches of the forbidden tree, and the entire order of their lives and nature are questioned.

"Did God really say, 'You must not eat from any tree in the garden'?"

The woman said to the serpent, "We may eat fruit from the trees in the garden, but God did say, 'You must not eat fruit from the tree that is in the middle of the garden, and you must not touch it, or you will die.'"

"You will not certainly die," the serpent said to the woman. "For God knows that when you eat from it your eyes will be opened, and you will be like God, knowing good and evil."

GENESIS 3:1-5

This deceitful idea planted by the serpent grew quickly. It suggested that God might not have told them the whole story, that He was withholding information He didn't want them to know. If they would eat this fruit they would be awakened to things only God knew and would be just like God.

Why would God put something like that tree in the Garden, in front of Adam and Eve? God created humankind in His own image and implanted a bit of Himself into each of us. He created something He called "very good." He created creatures who could know Him and be known by Him, creatures who could glorify Him and enjoy Him forever. He crafted something He loved dearly, and He desired that love to be returned. But love isn't something that can be forced upon another person. Authentic love makes a person vulnerable. Love isn't love if there's no way out. Maybe the tree was the way out.

But in this narrative, the evil one injected two devious concepts into God's picture of love—and into the human story. First, if God isn't telling you the whole story and is holding out on you, maybe there are other things He's keeping secret. And how can you trust someone who keeps secrets and tells you only what he wants you to know? Second, if you eat this you will be like God. Which is to say, you won't really need this God who keeps secrets from you anymore. You'll be your own god.

Haven't those themes prevailed over millennia? Aren't they the central themes that break up any relationship— that secrets are being kept and you're ultimately on your own? If you begin to live with those assumptions grafted into your heart and mind, then this is the lens you interpret everything through. The echoes of those messages are everywhere. If you think about it for a minute, you can probably find them deeply embedded in your own story. We've all been following the same script:

"God is sovereign and He does love you, but He's not completely reliable. You just don't know what He'll do. When push comes to shove, you have to be ready to act on your own because He might not come through."

God has basically been framed as the very wealthy uncle who also happens to be the family drunk. We need to keep Him happy so that we can get what we want and need, but we need to steer clear of His rages—and He's certainly not all that reliable. Staying on His good side gives us the generosity we want for our own lives, and we'll say whatever we think He wants to hear to get it. And what kind of relationship is that?

The irony is that God didn't eat the forbidden fruit or believe the lie. We did. So who is untrustworthy?

This view of God is the origin of all our assumption and mistrust. All the doubt and misunderstanding start here. And the suggestions inserted into the story by the evil one at that critical moment were like cancer cells injected into the image of God. His image in us and the way we see

Him haven't been the same since. And we can even turn to the tough stories in the Bible as a way of reinforcing the way we feel.

BIBLE HEARSAY

For most of my life I had an antagonistic relationship with the Bible. Before I was a pastor's son, I was the son of an evangelist. I spent my earliest childhood traveling around the countryside, living in a travel trailer behind whatever church was hosting my father's revival meetings.

In those days an evangelist's job was to preach weeklong evening services. Churchgoers would bring their unbelieving friends so that they could hear of the simple reality of an eternity with God—and also one without Him. As I recall, the messages about trumpet blasts and Jesus on a white horse splitting the sky open often terrified me. The room would light up with enthusiasm as we heard of the dead in Christ rising first to meet Him in the air, but my imagination ran wild.

At this point in my life I can process this message and find encouragement, but at eight years old I would lie in my bunk, considering that I might randomly be awakened by a horn and fly through the roof into the sky with a bunch of dead people. I couldn't sort out how I was going to get through the roof of the trailer without first being killed. And what would happen if I were stuck to the ceiling but couldn't get to Jesus? What if He were gone before the roof gave way? The whole matter was terribly confusing. But there was a worse alternative. *Not* flying into the sky at all. Being left behind, alone in a godless world.

In my confusion, I grew up believing that Jesus loved me but His Father was perpetually angry. In my adulthood I could not reconcile the two. The Bible became little more than the book that revealed the advanced failure of my faith. And this caused me to question everything about it.

It wasn't until I laid down all of my assumptions and came crawling to Scripture with no pretense or agenda that it began to unfold. When I came with open hands and an open heart to see if God could actually speak for Himself, I realized how much baggage I had heaped upon the Bible and how much hearsay I had believed about God.

One of the most compelling things about the Bible is that it doesn't shy away from messy things as if they will give God bad press, despite our human propensity toward mistrust and misunderstanding. It doesn't avoid real life. Life can be beautiful and pathetic all on the same day. We find in the Bible that God is present in all of it. He's not afraid of the messes we make. Lightning bolts are never His first reaction. He doesn't prefer judgment.

His first response is to redeem everything we allow Him to touch.

There are many points in Scripture that expose our hearts in this way, just as there are many circumstances in life that bare our heart's posture toward God. Continually monitoring the posture of our hearts in any relationship is important. In a successful relationship we choose to believe that our hearts are good toward each other. It's only when we doubt this that the relationship begins to go sideways with ill-advised assumptions. It's no different with God. We must believe that His heart is good toward us in order to trust Him, and this belief can only come from knowing Him and not just knowing a few things about Him. But this works both ways. Are our hearts good toward God? Are we reciprocating what is necessary for trust? Or are we choosing hearsay and assumption as the basis for relationship with Him while not being trustworthy in our own lives? If you were God, would you trust you?

But even with hearts that are good toward God, we can find the tough stories from Scripture hard to swallow. When we encounter a story in the Bible that is troubling or violent or even revolting, it can pick at all the assumptions and misconceptions we have about God's character like a scab. It can cause us to question whether He's someone we

can actually trust. How could God be involved with some
of these things? Let's try to locate God in these stories and
examine the jagged little assumptions in our hearts' posture toward Him while we're exploring.

Lot

The story of Abraham's nephew Lot has raised a few eye-
brows. It's the first place in Scripture we rub up against
something that doesn't quite feel right, no matter what
culture we live in.

> Afterward Lot left Zoar because he was afraid of
> the people there, and he went to live in a cave
> in the mountains with his two daughters. One day
> the older daughter said to her sister, "There are no
> men left anywhere in this entire area, so we can't
> get married like everyone else. And our father will
> soon be too old to have children. Come, let's get
> him drunk with wine, and then we will have sex
> with him. That way we will preserve our family
> line through our father."
>
> So that night they got him drunk with wine,
> and the older daughter went in and had intercourse
> with her father. He was unaware of her lying down
> or getting up again.

The next morning the older daughter said
to her younger sister, "I had sex with our father
last night. Let's get him drunk with wine again
tonight, and you go in and have sex with him.
That way we will preserve our family line through
our father." So that night they got him drunk with
wine again, and the younger daughter went in
and had intercourse with him. As before, he was
unaware of her lying down or getting up again.

As a result, both of Lot's daughters became
pregnant by their own father.

GENESIS 19:30-36, NLT

Seriously? Why is incest—girls having sex with their father—recorded in the Bible? Did you sense outrage and conflict in your heart as you read this passage? It's tough to juxtapose "God is hopelessly in love with you" with two daughters having sex with their dad. And it presses on those assumptions that cling to us from our own life stories. Little messages that say, "God can't be totally trusted, and neither can the Bible. Not for real. When the pressure is on, you are probably on your own."

So why is the story about Lot and his daughters in the Bible, and is there anything redeeming about it that has anything to do with us?

If we move back in the story just a bit, we'll find the patriarch Abraham standing with his nephew Lot on a bluff, looking out across the land. They'd been traveling together since they left their homeland in pursuit of the one true God, who had called Abraham from his home and told him to go to a land he would be shown. Traveling together in such close quarters and being constantly on the move had created tension.

Abraham told Lot that it was time they blessed each other and parted ways so the infighting would stop. He gave Lot the choice of which direction to head in, and Lot chose the Jordan valley, settling near the city of Sodom. Abraham went the opposite way and settled in Hebron.

God eventually decided to destroy Sodom and Gomorrah for their unspeakable wickedness and sent angels who found their way to Lot's house in Sodom. The city lived up to its wicked reputation. As men of the city surrounded Lot's home, demanding the visitors be turned over so they could be sexually abused, Lot pleaded with his fellow Sodomites to leave. He even offered them his two virgin daughters to be molested instead of his guests.

In the end the men were struck blind, and Lot was urgently rushed from the city with his family. His virgin daughters were betrothed, but their fiancés refused to leave the city, so the family escaped without them. Their instructions were to move with haste and not look back. Lot's wife didn't obey and lost her life in the process, which left only Lot and his daughters, who ended up hiding in a cave. This is how we arrive at the daughters' critical choice to try to get pregnant by their father.

Their mother is dead. Their fiancés are dead. The girls know how their father values them since he offered them for gang rape before Sodom was destroyed. They are living in a cave, hiding from the treacherous people of the valley. These are very young girls whose lives have taken a traumatic turn. They're probably about the age of high-school freshmen. They must have felt hopeless. Their father had lost everything and had no social standing to find suitable spouses for them. The likelihood of being raped and forced into prostitution was extremely high, and when their father died, his name would also die and there would be no heir left to claim or protect them. They were foreign girls. Their extended family was in a land too far away for them to return to. They decided that the only choice they had was to get him drunk and try to get pregnant. If they were successful and bore sons, the family name would continue and they would have some semblance of protection from the violent and evil culture they lived in.

Why didn't they flee to their great-uncle Abraham in Hebron? We don't know. Probably for the same reason they were hiding in a cave. Why did God let this happen? That's the big question, isn't it?

It's easy to get sucked into a story like this. We put ourselves in their position and leap to judgment. But if we review the text, there are a couple of fascinating absences. First, we don't find any place where God instructed this, condoned it, or required it. He didn't. And second, we never see Lot or his daughters considering the God whom their family left its homeland to follow.

We read a passage like this and for some reason blame God, even though God had nothing to do with it. God rescued Lot and his daughters from the judgment falling on an unspeakably cruel, perverted, and merciless city. His role was that of the Redeemer. What came next was a result of the systematic choices of the people involved.

Why would God let something like this happen? Remember the tree in the garden? We're allowed to make choices. God doesn't circumnavigate that gift of freedom. *Love isn't love if there's no way out.* We can choose whatever we want to do, and at any point we can choose Him. He will begin to redeem whatever He's allowed to touch. But we bear the weight of our decisions. This is the dignity of a free will—and the dignity required for authentic relationship. This is one of the ways we are created in God's image.

Who is untrustworthy in this story? God? No. He saved

Lot and his family from certain destruction. Lot's daughters chose to take matters into their own hands, believing they were on their own and no one was coming to rescue them, even after God had sent angels they could see with their own eyes to get them out of the city.

To believe that in some way God is an uncertain ally is to limit our ability to give ourselves to Him completely. How can you truly love someone you don't trust? How can a relationship ever work that way? And, as we talked about earlier, this was exactly what was injected into our story so long ago: that God keeps secrets. He can't be trusted fully. You need to take matters into your own hands.

STOP BLAMING GOD FOR HUMAN CHOICES

We've been created in the image of God and given the ability to make choices of our own free will, just like the choice Adam and Eve made at the tree in the Garden. To eat the forbidden fruit was a choice. And God allowed it. He allows us to make choices, and He allows those choices to matter. Again, *love isn't love if there's no way out*. When I said earlier that it's all about you and all about what you do next, I wasn't kidding.

We make hundreds of choices each day, and it's easy to consider that these choices are insignificant or only affect us. Even when we're faced with a decision that feels weighty, we still believe that it probably only affects us and perhaps a small circle of others.

But everything matters. Everything we do and say carries significant potential. If we were to approach life with this in mind, we might pause and realize we are part of a much larger and interconnected story, a story that we can't hope to navigate on our own. We can demand freedoms that we aren't equipped to wield without guidance, and the outcomes can be devastating. We're made to walk with God.

We can't blame God for men selling underage girls for sex in Moldova or a crazed person walking into a Colorado movie theater with firearms or people flying airplanes into buildings in New York or tribes hacking one another to pieces in Rwanda. We can't wrap our minds around some of these evils, so we look to God for answers. Perhaps God is looking to us and asking, "Why are you doing this? Why are you letting this happen?" This is far more true to Scripture than the way the evil one framed God in Genesis 3 and the way we've been looking at Him ever since.

The choices we make in every relationship matter, including the ones in our relationship with God. All of our choices matter. We create the world we live in with our choices just as God created the world and gave it to us as a gift to steward. We bear the image of our creator God individually and collectively as humankind, and we are constantly creating our destinies. We each have a role to play.

Do people get to make their choices and take the consequences? Certainly. We can be our own gods, carrying around all our knowledge of good and evil. This was the trade made in the Garden. But we can't have it both ways. We can't demand our freedom on one hand while blaming God for our actions and their repercussions on the other. It's completely unfair to blame God for our own unfaithfulness.

The way we've framed God has been wrong. It's made the picture we have of Him incorrect and incomplete. We have a Father who is trustworthy, kind, and eternal, and we traded a perfect relationship with Him for the knowledge of good and evil. Even as a chasm of betrayal was carved between Him and His creation, God never abandoned us. He continues to pursue us. Through covenants, judges, and the lone voices of prophets, He continued to come for His people. And through the power of His Holy Spirit and His Word and the gift of His own Son, He continues to come for us.

PART TWO
REFRAME

*If we create our worldview, we can re-create it too by
taking a different perspective and reframing our situation.*

KEN ROBINSON,
THE ELEMENT

*What you are must always displease you, if you would
attain to that which you are not.*

SAINT AUGUSTINE OF HIPPO

Chapter 4

REFRAMING STARVATION

I didn't set out to discover Truth. I was simply hungry and
digging deep in the back of the fridge and boom! there it was.
And I've got to tell you, the Truth was tasty.

JAROD KINTZ,
THE DAYS OF YAY ARE HERE!

Our fall was, has always been, and always will be,
that we aren't satisfied in God and what He gives.
We hunger for something more, something other.

ANN VOSKAMP,
ONE THOUSAND GIFTS

BROWN EYES

Several years ago, I was in India teaching a two-week class
to aspiring artists. I had been warned in advance that
India has a way of getting under your skin. This proved
to be an understatement. Never have I wandered into a
culture so different in nearly every way from the one I
was raised in. The faint smell of charcoal fires permeat-
ing the entire atmosphere is still vivid in my memory. I
clearly see the vast throngs of colorful people dressed in

everything from the traditional sari or dhoti and kurta to Levis and a turban. Traffic laws seemed optional, and fruit, vegetables, and freshly cut flowers were as ubiquitous as piles of refuse. Wandering cows lapped water lazily from the public fountains. I recall Hindu idol worship in the marketplaces and trucks of squawking chickens on their way to being dinner. I consumed a lifetime's worth of rice and naan. But for as long as I live, I will never forget the chance encounter I had in the middle of a bustling business district.

Traveling after any fashion in India felt dodgy, and not knowing any of the common tongues left me feeling isolated. I never gathered the courage to wander alone, but when I needed to restock on supplies or sit in an Internet café, someone would graciously accompany me. The fastest way to maneuver India's city streets is by motorcycle or rickshaw, and on this day we were traveling by the latter. I had been enjoying the wind in my face and sensory overload when traffic halted us and every horn began to blow simultaneously.

From the corner of my eye I saw her walking toward me—an extraordinarily beautiful Indian girl with enormous brown eyes. In any other context I would have thought her a professional model, but she was barefoot and wore a tattered blue dress.

She approached me with hand outstretched, softly calling, "Sir." When I faced her I was again struck by her beauty and frailty. She took her open hand and brought it to her mouth and then again extended her open palm toward me. She was asking for money so that she could eat. I melted. I was prepared to empty my pockets into her open palm.

"They are everywhere," said my companion in the thick Indian accent I was becoming accustomed to. "Everywhere the children are begging for money—especially from Westerners. You must look forward and ignore her and she will leave you alone. If you don't, it will only get worse. More will come. You will be mobbed."

I faced my friend. "How can I not help her? How does this happen?"

As this beautiful girl kept beckoning me, he told me of the many children who grow up on their own this way. Their parents abandon them or die, and there is no mechanism inside the culture or government to care for them. They're sometimes exploited. Many find street families who give them protection but also send them into populated areas to beg each day.

I sat facing forward as instructed while the knot in my throat threatened to choke me. A cloud of hopeless loneliness had descended on this beautiful afternoon.

I was deeply conflicted inside. How could I not help in any way I could? But how could anything I gave bring any sort of true change to her life? Tears welled behind my hundred-dollar sunglasses. I was face-to-face with a crisis of the heart.

I looked at her and told her I was sorry. She didn't understand me. Her response was to say, "Please," and once again she brought her hand to her mouth and pulled it away, facing me like a judge pronouncing a sentence.

About the time I decided to reach into my pocket again, the traffic broke free and we began to move. "Please sir," she said, but then we were gone. I turned to look back and saw this beautiful girl with her big brown eyes staring at me from the middle of the motorway while traffic engulfed her. I felt like I had just left Jesus hungry on the street, and I didn't know what to do with myself.

Hunger is an interesting thing. Because it's not just something experienced in our stomach. This encounter left me feeling emptier than my stomach could have ever been.

HUNGRY

Hunger drives nearly everything we do. Anger, power, revenge, love, and even faith are driven by the same single thing: hunger. Hunger shapes our lives, and at the center of it all is the longing of the soul. We may not articulate it in these terms or acknowledge the longing at all, but denying it won't change it. This is how we are made. The emptiness we often feel in life and the craving that lingers at the heart of us is a deep longing for meaning waiting to be filled. And there is no way to get there without a living, breathing, moment-by-moment, collaborative connection to the source of life itself.

I tried just about everything imaginable to find lasting fulfillment. You probably have too. I also know that no matter what I accomplished or achieved, it was not enough. I masked it through copious amounts of activity and a reckless pace for over two decades in the music industry, but though I pursued and achieved goals that very few people ever get to experience, it was still not enough. I was starving inside, and it was a spiritual hunger I didn't know how to fill.

A starving person will eat just about anything—shoe leather, dirt mixed with rotten flesh, anything that will provide even the illusion of nourishment. And we will do the same spiritually, even though we might not realize what we're doing. We're all starving for life because we're made to have it. And life can only be found the way it was designed—in collaboration with God.

THE GREAT DISCONNECT

We'd all agree that sustenance is desperately needed for a malnourished and wasted body. Once a body has burned away its fat stores and consumed all its muscle tissue, the vital organs are the only things left to turn into fuel. A body will sustain life as long as it can, but there comes a point when, without nutrition, the starving body will shut down. Life will end, leaving behind an emaciated corpse.

Fuel is necessary to support life, and fuel is found in food. To regenerate the body and restore itself, the body needs significant complex nutrition. A person can certainly survive awhile on whatever passes for "food," but to create a healthy and restorative environment, the body needs the sort of nutrition that it knows what to do with. It needs to turn the nutritious food into fuel to run the system that sustains life. Although we accept this as biological fact, it's remarkable how easily we ignore the spiritual implications. Like our physical bodies, our spirits also need nutrition.

We've talked a lot about life being a precious gift. But this gift—whether in body or in spirit—is ours to steward, and we sustain it through the nourishment we provide to it. Probably we would agree that the soul's nutrition is found in a connection or relationship with God. In the first part of this book, we dismantled many of the things that either blur this connection or distort it. Now let's figure out why we're in this malnourished state, because it's only a matter of time before we will begin to wither.

THE SHAPE OF REALITY

Take a moment to consider: What words would you use to describe your life during the last couple of years? For most people, life is a bit of a blur—a constant struggle to avoid hardship and achieve some sort of balance, all while maintaining a heart of gratitude. Everything feels as if it's moving too fast, and some form of anxiety or depression stalks one step behind us as we run and run and run toward whatever is dangled in front of us.

Beneath the constant motion, doesn't something often feel empty? As if we're running from something but not really toward anything? Often, we're just trying to outrun whatever we think might happen to us if we stop.

And layered on top of this, there's the posturing that, truthfully, makes us feel like isolated imposters. Everyone else seems to be further along. Everyone else seems to have it more together. We feel like we're falling further and further behind. Our hopes and dreams seem further out of reach. It feels pretty much as if we're failing at life. As if we're reading a book that we began in the middle. The plot isn't clear—just a blur of characters moving in intricate patterns. And as interesting and colorful as everything might be, none of it makes much sense.

With the constant struggle to outrun whatever is nipping at our heels and the added pressure of trying to keep up with everyone who seems to be outpacing us, we end up putting on a happy face, carrying around our religious clichés, doubling up on our efforts to check off the list of things we read in a book somewhere that promised fulfillment, and trying to study more about God so He won't be even more angry at us than He already is. But none of these things actually move us toward intimacy.

The great nineteenth-century writer and preacher Charles Spurgeon said, "No one is so miserable as the poor person who maintains the appearance of wealth." It's all just exhausting, isn't it? It can feel as if we're being herded along like cattle. And the haunting fear is that if we slow the whole thing down and take time to reflect, life is going to be exactly as King Solomon described it: "Utterly meaningless! Everything is meaningless. What do people gain from all their labors at which they toil under the sun?" (Ecclesiastes 1:2-3).

This is what spiritual hunger feels like. This is the starvation of the soul. It affects every other relationship and every other part of our lives. And to really understand this hunger, we have to acknowledge that everything starts with our wrong frame around God.

CONSUMABLE

Hunger itself isn't a bad thing once we understand it. It drives us and forces us into action. Action that matters and expresses itself in the myriad choices we make every single day. I've said that this is all about you and all about what you do next. Never has this been more true than when it comes to hunger.

Hunger shapes our lives. In other words, our lives are in the shape they are in because of how we choose to fill our hunger. As believers we have been told that only God can fill our hunger for life. It's an overused cliché of our faith. But do we actually believe this? Is God actually filling the hunger of our lives? Because if He is, why are we still hungry?

In our marketing-driven society we're told that any given product or service we buy will fill our hunger. It's so pervasive that, without realizing it, we can even become consumers when it comes to our relationships.

God isn't a product that can fill us any more than our husbands or wives are. When we attempt to use Him this way it doesn't work because *we're using Him*. You may have experienced a relationship in your life in which you felt used. Likely you are not still involved in that relationship, and you probably don't have fond memories of it. We can't be users in our relationship with God any more than we can successfully foster a life-giving relationship with another person by using and consuming them.

MARRIAGE

In Scripture, marriage is often used to describe our relationship with God. But often we look at it so allegorically that we miss how present and disruptive this metaphor really is.

Relating to our spouse and being in a relationship with God have surprisingly deep similarities. It is as if God embedded a road map in our physical lives to remind us of how deep our union is with Him and how invested we have to be in that union for it to work.

Marriage is hard. Let's just get that out of the way. It's hard because it carries within it the most sacred and significant potential in the world, and it has to be contended for as the gift it is. The union we have with our spouse is something we often don't treat that way—as sacred—and the intimacy we crave is something we're usually not completely willing to chase after because of what it's going to cost us. We often think that getting into a marriage will make things better in our lives, only to find out that this is not true.

Or is it? What a marriage requires of two individuals is that they be willing to commingle their lives every single moment for the rest of their lives so that in the end the two of them become one. This is not easy. It's painful and difficult and constant. But for those who finally break through and glimpse what is happening, it's also the most transcendent and fulfilling thing life has to offer.

A troubled relationship is one that has forgotten what it is—a miracle. When two people can carry all of their history and assumptions, their dreams and nightmares, their wills and their bodies into a supercollider and choose to slam them together at warp speed so that something new and better can be created, it's a miracle. But many of us are unwilling to be made new—and this is what is required. We go into the marriage looking for a more complete "I," not realizing that for this to happen, "I" has to be remade into "we."

In this environment of expectations, the work of relationship carves ruts. Negotiated truces create resentment and misunderstanding, so we attempt to compartmentalize and seek life outside the relationship. It doesn't have to be adultery. It's just the subtle giving of our hearts to something else. We're hungry for life, and if we're not getting what we want or need, we attempt to feed ourselves in other ways. Before long we've forgotten what we dreamed of being together. We've forgotten the miracle we are together. The delicate dance of power and respect leaves us trapped behind battle lines we're not willing to surrender anymore.

But what a marriage relationship requires every single day of its existence is actually less complicated than we make it. Ultimately it simply requires that we both act in love. Acting in unconditional love means that we pursue rather than withdraw even if it means surrender. We disrupt the status quo. We attack a problem and not each other. Our north star is that we believe our hearts are good toward each other. We need to be willing to give ourselves to each other utterly and completely and to rescue each other. What "we" need is more important than what "I" need. We are supposed to lay our lives down for each other in life and, if necessary, in death.

Every single word of the promises we make on our wedding day—and then some—will be required to make it work. And both people have to be willing to act with the same reckless abandon for each other, knowing that the unity being created is sacred and holy and unstoppable until death separates them. If both spouses aren't simultaneously acting in love, life will drain from the relationship.

This is what it takes to find life in a marriage—and what it takes to find life with God. It's hard work to let "I" go for the sake of "we." It's the constant subversion of every selfish and ghastly thing within us. Some of these things don't die easily. But it is this sort of commitment to a connection with our Creator that can finally fill the hunger—from the inside out.

INSIDE OUT . . .

We have to begin by understanding that true life radiates from inside us—from our hearts outward. We cannot feed our soul's hunger from the outside. If we're not acknowledging this and constantly aware of it, life can be much like driving an automobile forward while looking through the rearview mirror. Everything feels backward, and our orientation to where we're headed is dangerously impaired. No matter how careful we try to be, we will eventually crash. The Scriptures tell us, "Above all else, guard your heart, for everything you do flows from it" (Proverbs 4:23), but in so many tangible ways this is the last thing we do. We're seduced into believing that exterior pleasure is what provides inner peace. But this is not true. It's a devastating and dangerous fallacy.

Jesus talked about this when He spoke to the religious

leaders about the way they were maintaining the illusion: "You are like whitewashed tombs, which look beautiful on the outside but on the inside are full of the bones of the dead and everything unclean" (Matthew 23:27).

When we live trying to fill from the outside what is empty inside us, it exacerbates the problem just as eating empty calories actually makes us hungrier. Running from one external source to another in an effort to fill our lives with pleasure and comfort won't fill the emptiness that lingers inside. In the end we don't have a larger life full of meaning; we have a smaller one full of obligation.

. . . NOT OUTSIDE IN

To flee the smaller life, we must reframe how we attempt to achieve wholeness by taking stock of how well our lives are being lived from the inside out. But we must also reframe the external circumstances that seem to fly at us faster than we can process. Considering the information we are required to process in a day and separating it into two piles—one that reads "Life and Death" and another that reads "Nonessential for Life"—can be a necessary awakening to how distracted and compartmentalized we live. We give much of our precious lives to nonessential things. Usually we're running too fast and hard to be aware that we don't have to live this way. The compounding motion of life becomes an addiction that we feed constantly. But the time that we have to live within our humanity is finite and priceless. Compared to eternity, it is but a wisp or a vapor. Here today and then gone (James 4:14)—and yet we give this priceless treasure to things that don't deserve such a high price. We burn through the currency of our days, spending them on cheap imitations.

You'll also have to be awakened to the fact that all this addiction to motion and activity—the very things that leave you exhausted and confused about the meaning of it all at the end of the year—are your attempts to feed your starving soul. You may consume any number of things to feel full. But being full isn't the same as being nourished.

If you aren't quite sure that you need to fight for what has been stolen from you, perhaps a critical assessment of what is taking your life away would be worthwhile. You will see that, although you consciously give yourself to things that don't matter, there are many things that are stealing life from you, and you can never get it back. Once life is burned through, it's gone. You cannot relive a day. God can restore life and can give us back what has been wasted (Joel 2:25), but you'll have to identify what—and who—is stealing it from you first.

EXPOSING THE THIEF

Jesus came so we could experience this larger life. But that's only half of what He was saying. He first told us "the thief comes only to steal and kill and destroy" (John 10:10). We're going to have to believe Him. We must acknowledge that our outside world will not have meaning until our inside life is nourished. The easiest way for the thief to rob you isn't to outright assault you. It's to attempt to sell you an imitation in exchange for your precious life. This thief will, if given the chance, steal the nourishment our souls crave and sabotage our relationship with God in any way we'll allow.

If we believed this one truth, really believed that we have a mortal enemy, it would serve as another large piece of the puzzle. So many things in life would make sense. Hasn't it often felt like life was being stolen from you? Like you're being slowly destroyed? And all the while we either blame circumstances or shake our fists in God's face, assuming it's His fault, when there is an evil one who is not only stealing our lives but also getting away with it. We must be willing to fight to take back what has been stolen.

Imagine you've just left the mall. The sun has set and the sky has quieted to deepest indigo. As you carry your purchases to the car you notice the stars twinkling and the tender breeze on your face. Preoccupied, you don't notice the man until it's too late. He's upon you, wrapping gloved hands around your neck. A stiff knee to your kidneys sends you to the ground, bags flying out in front of you. The parking lot pavement bites into your cheek. There's blood in your mouth. Old motor oil stains your clothing a filthy brown, but blackness is coming. His chokehold is blocking your ability to gasp for breath. If you could speak you'd offer your keys, your money—whatever he wants. But in utter disbelief you realize that what he wants is your life. And he's taking it.

What are you going to do? Die not understanding why? Blame God for letting this happen? Feel a deep sense of depression and betrayal over what could have been? Or will you writhe and claw and bite and scratch? Wouldn't you kick and scream and squirm and shriek, doing whatever it takes to stay alive? We all want to live.

We'd struggle with every fiber of our beings as we focused on our spouses and children. We'd muster strength we didn't know we had. We'd do whatever it took to stay alive. We wouldn't lie there and say, "Jesus, I just ask that you make this all go away," or "God, why is this happening to me?" We would fight to the death.

And this is a fair picture of the resolve it's going to take. There is a thief and a destroyer stalking us, attempting to steal away every morsel of nutrition that would give us life. We have to believe that he would steal our lives from us if permitted. We have to be willing to draw the line here, before the next page, and decide that those days are over. We have to be willing to fight to get our lives back.

Are you finally realizing that much of what you've been experiencing is simply hunger, and that there is a thief who is constantly looking for the opportunity to steal any nourishment from you? This realization leads to questions: How do I develop an honest collaborative relationship with God? How can I fight this starvation? Where am I going to find the nourishment I need?

Chapter 5

REFRAMING NOURISHMENT

If we could give every individual the right amount of
nourishment and exercise, not too little and not too much,
we would have found the safest way to health.

HIPPOCRATES

When it comes to literal nourishment,
the food we eat, life begets life.

VICTORIA MORAN,
"AGELESS LIVING IN A CULTURE OF YOUTH"

Once we're clear that we're facing spiritual starvation, we begin to understand how desperately we need God and how deeply we are created to be with Him and He with us in an intimate, personal, and life-giving relationship. If our hearts are the wellspring of life and we grant access to this central part of who we are to God, we are connecting to life itself. And Jesus promises, "Everyone who drinks this water will be thirsty again, but whoever drinks the water I give them will never thirst. Indeed, the water I give them will become in them a spring of water welling up to eternal life" (John 4:13-14).

A never-off, always-on, moment-by-moment friend-ship with God connects us at the core of who we are to the very source of life. From this source, life can radiate outward into everything that we do and say—every thought, word, and deed. Life comes bursting out of us, touching every other relationship we have and shaping our lives accordingly. Exterior circumstances no longer dictate how we experience life because they don't have access to our hearts any longer. Our relationship with God overwhelms what is exterior, changing the shape of how we live. And in the midst of our starvation, we begin to find nourishment.

SHALOM

What would it look like if you lived a fully nourished life? It's not as simple of a question as it initially seems, is it? We generally begin with all the circumstances in our lives we would like to see removed or changed. It's the outside-in versus inside-out life we spoke of in the last chapter. We're indoctrinated by a severely market-driven culture to believe that if we could get our outside world in some sort of balance by purchasing the right products and ser-vices, we would have inner peace or at least have time to explore it. But the reverse is actually true. Life radiates from within, and we'll never find external order without a nourished soul.

There is an ancient Hebrew word that deeply resonates within the Jewish culture. The word is *shalom*. Usually we hear this word and immediately think of *peace*, which is typically the word-for-word translation into English. But a word-for-word translation sometimes does not do full justice to the complete meaning. *Love*, for example, means many things, but in its purest form can only be found in the deepest core of our beings where language, science, and logic can no longer fully explain its reality. *Shalom* is like this. It really does mean peace, but it's a certain kind of peace. And it is more than peace. A better word would probably be *wholeness*.

If you're thinking about what it might look and feel like to be spiritually nourished, you'll wind up with the ancient word *shalom*. It's what we earnestly desire and what we're made for. *Shalom* speaks of purest joy. It speaks of wholeness and completeness in a place of truth and justice. It is safety and soundness and forgiveness and security. It is God's perfect order in all things, at all times, and in all places. Author Cornelius Plantinga beautifully describes *shalom* as "*universal flourishing, wholeness, and delight*—a rich state of affairs in which natural needs are satisfied and natural gifts fruitfully employed, a state of affairs that inspires joyful wonder as its Creator and Savior opens doors and welcomes the creatures in whom he delights. *Shalom*, in other words, is the way things ought to be."[1]

This is what it looks and feels like to be spiritually nourished, and it cannot be achieved externally. It must be created and cultivated from within. We cannot purchase enough items to generate it within us or accomplish enough that we might have it. External devices simply invite us to measure how well we are doing compared to someone else. *Shalom* answers the question of how we are doing compared to our Creator's hope for us individually. You see, it really is all about you. God really does care enough to dream that you will find who you really are. And who you really are can only be found in a relationship with Him.

Although there are many fundamental elements involved in a nourished relationship, two are irreplaceable. The first is identity, which we find in the Word of God. If we don't know who we are, we don't have ourselves to offer in relationship with anyone. The second is communication. It's not possible to grow intimately without offering ourselves, and this is done through communication with God through prayer. This may seem obvious. But maybe it doesn't work quite the way we think it does.

IDENTITY

The little church seemed nothing like it had been described. The dilapidated exterior was falling apart. It looked as if it had been abandoned for years. There was a large opening where the front doors would have stood. I stepped across creaking boards and into the interior, hoping not to meet a rattlesnake. This tiny country church was the place where it all began for me. It was the spot where my father, as a boy of eight, knelt in prayer and gave his life to God.

I'd heard of this place all my life, but I had never been inside it. The story of my father finding his Savior was mythic in my mind, but the rotting carpet, ancient paneling, and empty shell of a sanctuary was far from storybook. The old cross hanging from the wall caught my attention. I envisioned where an altar would have been and imagined my father as a little boy kneeling in prayer.

Across the street and just beyond the cemetery stands the one-room schoolhouse where my father attended. His body is now in the cemetery. He wanted to conclude his earthly journey where it began.

That little boy, in love with his mother and respectful of his rough-edged father, knelt with his aunt in that country church. My father would grow to love the Scriptures and eventually be called by God to ministry. His first church would be far away in rural Michigan, where he would fall in love with my mother. The worlds of Scotland and Poland collided to create me. Later I would feel the same pull toward ministry.

It's fascinating how we get to where we are. There's a bit of serendipity, a bit of faith, and a lot of what only appears to be random. All the decisions that my father made after kneeling in that country church conspired to help form me into the man I was to become. And although the little church seemed nothing like I had envisioned, I felt the most profound sense of identity when standing inside its walls.

Hasn't the search for identity been one of the central themes of your life? Without identity there is no way to move in any direction with any sense of purpose. And it seems as if we lose track of our spiritual identity about as often as we misplace our keys.

When we lose a spiritual sense of who we are, we can only compare ourselves to others. This forces us back to life from the outside in, which leaves an insatiable hunger at our core. Keeping connected to our identity is probably the greatest source of nourishment the Scriptures offer. It's like an intravenous hookup to spiritual life. Knowing our identity is the key to everything. If we forget who we are, we're lost in just about every conceivable way. The Bible is a gift that tangibly connects us to our spiritual heritage. Identity is bestowed within its pages, which allows us to come into a nourishing relationship with God as we learn who and what we are.

What if I told you that the Bible is more about you than it is about God? Would that shock you? It sounds a bit sacrilegious, doesn't it? But stay with me here. If God had wanted to write a book *about* Himself *for* Himself, it's highly unlikely we'd understand a word of it. Would it even be written with words? Is God bound to the awkward, clumsy, oft-misunderstood use of language? Does He need grammar in order to communicate, or is it we who need it? For that matter, does God need the Bible? Probably not. But we need it desperately because the Bible is the narrative that tells us where we've come from. It gives us our identity. And knowing who we are is the only way to offer ourselves in an intimate and nourishing relationship.

When I was a young man coming of age, my father told me how important it was to know my roots and not forget that I carried our family name. Although I didn't honor that advice as thoroughly as I now wish, I never forgot it either. It means more to me now than ever before. Knowing where you've come from and who your family is—even if you'd rather forget—profoundly informs the decisions you make and convictions you hold. It's planted deep within you. It orients you to where you're headed and connects you to a larger story. The story that brought you to this point in time flows through thousands of years and millions of decisions by your forebearers. Many random things have happened along the way, but there is a pattern to it all—and it has led you here to this page right now. Think about that for a minute. It took a lot of work and many decisions to place you here at this very moment. And those choices were made by people you are related to but may never have met or even heard of.

The Bible is the story of your spiritual heritage. Your spiritual heritage has as significant of an influence in your life as your family tree ever will, and there is no separating that story from the God who is interwoven throughout. Seeing the patterns of God's involvement in human endeavors reveals how clearly He wants to be involved and collaborating in your life. The Bible is your story. It's all about you and all about what you do next. The story isn't over.

GOD WITH US

In composing the Scriptures God did what He's always done—He inspired people. God inspired the Bible *through* people. Why? God didn't need people in order to create the Scriptures. Or did He? Because what we find in the Bible are fascinating stories about people and what happened to them based on the decisions they made.

Inspiration is simply causing something to be created. God has always chosen to collaborate with people. He doesn't have to do this, but it appears He wants to. Even after He became one of us in the person of Jesus, He still chose inspiration to complete the biblical narratives. God desires a life-giving and collaborative relationship with us—He wants to be near us (James 4:8). The entire biblical narrative shows God's remarkable desire to be among us. Isaiah 7 and the foretelling of the Savior illustrate how profoundly this is embedded in Scripture. Jesus is called Immanuel—God *with* us. God has constantly fought for the relationship He desires *with* us, and the Bible tells the story inspired by God but lived through humanity. It's impossible to separate God from people and people from God in Scripture. If you take either one out of the Bible, there is no Bible. The Bible gives us a sense of connectedness and identity in an ongoing story, and—as I said earlier—knowing who we are is necessary to entering into a collaborative and nourishing relationship with anyone, including God.

From the book of Genesis through the book of Revelation,

the Scriptures are the story of God *with* us. The interesting thing is that God doesn't need this story written down so He won't forget it. We do. God has spent thousands of years moving in and out of cultures and customs and looking through the eyes of humanity to reveal Himself through humanity. No matter where we are on this planet or what time period we find ourselves in, He connects us to the ongoing story. And if that weren't enough, He came in human form to be *with* us. He came to insert Himself into our story so profoundly that nothing has been the same since.

Jesus—God in human form—lived among us for three decades. If the purpose of His coming were simply to shed His innocent blood on our behalf so that our sins might be atoned for, He could have done that immediately. There's a point in the Christmas story when King Herod chose to kill the male children two years old and younger in fear of the coming King. Jesus could have been killed during the massacre, and His innocent, sinless blood would have been shed—but God chose to remain among us. He stayed here to be *with* us and show us what life is supposed to look like. When Jesus was preparing to depart Earth and return to the Father, He gave final instructions that we should go and tell everyone the Good News. This is known as the Great Commission. The great co-mission.

Something we do in collaboration together with God and with each other.

We need a clear understanding that our connection to God is something He really wants. He wants to be with us. Contained in the Scriptures are thousands of years of examples in a myriad of cultural contexts that show us how intensely committed God is to maintaining the relationship. We find a God who is recklessly in love with His people. Crazy in love. Hopelessly in love. It's impossible to miss it. But when we're disconnected from this source—His Word—we soon begin to forget our identity and hunger again. We hunger for life, so we buy whatever promises life, no matter how false the claims. We hunger for identity, so we compare ourselves to each other to get a sense of it. We hunger for intimacy and relationship, so we try to force unrealistic expectations on one another.

Hunger is an all-consuming motivator. We devour whatever is available to satisfy it, even if it's poison to our souls. The irony is that what we're starving for is available. We can be nourished by this deep sense of connection and relationship to what is greater than us and by the hope that there is peace and order in all things—*shalom*. And a primary source of that nourishment is the Bible.

REFRAMING THE BIBLE

If we're going to find nourishment in the Word of God, we have to reframe our picture and understanding of the Bible. It's not only a book of history or theology. It's not simply a book of rules that show how you're failing. It's not a leadership manual or the steps you must take to have marital bliss. It's not God's autobiography—as if a book could be written about an eternal, everlasting being who is beyond time and space and the mortal wisdom of men. The Bible is more than all of that. The Bible is the story of us—and God with us. It covers the complete arc of every emotion, struggle, conflict, and victory. It's love and hate and betrayal and redemption and denial and acceptance and misunderstanding and wholeness and indifference and rescue and confusion and doubt and empathy and suffering and regret and pleasure and homesickness and envy and euphoria and hope and gratitude and forgiveness.

The Bible is full of your life and the life of every other human being who has ever lived, with God in the middle of it as He always has been. As He inspired people to write these things down, He made sure that we have access to who we are, who He is, and how passionate He is to be *with* us. Do you want to be nourished? Reframe how you look at the Bible.

Listen and Return

You may say, "But the Bible isn't that easy to understand!" And therein lies its beauty. What we experience on any given day is full of drama and intrigue. When we wake up each morning, we have no idea what encounters and choices will come our way. We like to think we can order and control everything, but we can't. And that's part of the problem. We try to arrange for life—to create on our own a sense of *shalom*—but it is impossible to do without God in the middle of it. The Scriptures demonstrate every conceivable attempt to make life work, both as individuals and as societies, without God involved. It reveals where those pathways lead and their consequences. All the while it reveals a loving God who practically gets down on His knees and begs His people to listen and return to Him so that they can avoid the devastating storms they are headed into. God's Word could save us an enormous amount of floundering if we would give it the place of a counselor or trusted friend. It would keep us oriented and awake and aware of what is really going on inside of us if we would simply listen without prejudice.

Proper Posture

Although we can search the Scriptures from many perspectives when we're looking for orientation to God and spiritual nourishment, we're usually looking for clarity and purpose for today. We often approach the Bible as if it's a massive book of instructions and ethics (about as riveting as the federal code for business taxes), or we come to it with a scalpel and try to dissect it like we're in a science lab. Neither of those will be fulfilling if we don't see it first as a narrative, a complete story told with an open hand of friendship and counsel. We often try to parse the Bible completely differently from how we would engage any other narrative, much as we've approached a relationship with God in ways that would never work in any other relationship. Digging deeper into every aspect of Scripture isn't the problem. Trying to do it without first understanding the complete narrative is. It's like attempting brain surgery after having watched one operation on YouTube. Understanding the narrative and overarching themes is vital to finding nourishment and identity in the Bible. Only then can we successfully understand how to go deeper.

When we communicate, the words we choose transfer pictures and emotion and conflict and release. The words are the vehicle that communicates the life experience in a way that we can feel and connect with. We're not having a conversation while simultaneously attempting to diagram each other's sentences. If we approach the Bible only to parcel it out and dissect it, we're losing connection to the life the narrative brings. We must approach the Bible understanding that it first appeals to the deeper spaces in our hearts, the places beyond words. It tells us what is true all the way to our core.

The writer of Hebrews says it like this:

> The word of God is alive and active. Sharper
> than any double-edged sword, it penetrates even
> to dividing soul and spirit, joints and marrow;
> it judges the thoughts and attitudes of the heart.
>
> HEBREWS 4:12

The words of the Scriptures aren't there just to transfer data using the medium of language. They are there to awaken our hearts to what is true and challenge what is false. It's not just the language itself; it's what God awakens in our hearts because of the language. This is no different from any other mode of communication. But Scripture takes a deep dive into why we do what we do. It pulls no punches. It tells us the truth. There is no way to flinch away from it as we do when we're rationalizing our behavior to everyone, including ourselves. The Bible shows where we're heading, and we get to decide if that's the place we want to end up. It gives us identity and context for the relationship God has offered us.

When we come to the Bible, we must first come without any agenda other than to orient ourselves to God and let the words be His words to us. If it's His Word and our story, then there is rich wisdom and complex nourishment there. Don't approach it as a discipline you're supposed to adhere to. Leave behind the idea that it's a magic book of mantras to get you out of trouble and keep you safe. Don't even come for its inspiring literature. Come as if it's simpler than all the layers of complexity we heap upon it. If it's God's Word, then these are the things He wants to say to people through people. Once we understand the fundamental story that has unfolded over thousands of years, we begin to realize that the story isn't over and our lives are the continuation of it. We find our place in it. Then we have a platform to dive much deeper into the nuances and work out our own salvation with deep reverence and caution (Philippians 2:12).

If God desperately wants this relationship and deeply wants us to be aware of who we are, why would He cloak the whole thing in mystery so that we can't possibly understand? Rather than forcing us to hunt for all the nuances, perhaps the Scriptures speak to all the nuances of our lives. If we come with open hearts, God will speak to us. But the frame we often put the Bible in is probably the wrong one, just as we've often done with our relationship with God.

The Long Story

I'm not attempting to oversimplify the complexities of the Bible. But I am trying to reveal that, underneath the layers of theology and history and prophecy, the Bible is a narrative. The Bible is a story—a story about us, and God *with* us. Knowing this is paramount. Reframing our picture of the Bible makes all the difference. The heart of man has not changed much. Culture has changed drastically. Customs have come and gone, and technology has made the world an interconnected place in ways that the chroniclers of the Scriptures could have never imagined. But this has always been happening. Consider the fact that fifteen years ago there wasn't a Facebook or Twitter—we all see how rapidly our culture can change. But the hearts of humans and their search for love, meaning, and identity remain unchanged. And it is the understanding of these things that nourishes us spiritually.

The Bible is the long and continuing story of a God who will not surrender what He sees as precious and of a people who get to make their own decisions and live with them. It provides us a context for the story we are living in, and it gives us a mirror by which to look at ourselves. Without a mirror we don't know what we look like. And there is much to discover when we face ourselves in that mirror—every pore and freckle illuminated by the presence of the

Almighty—and find that He is still completely devoted and committed to loving us. We see that He really does want to be *with* us. We begin to realize that we really can be naked and unashamed with Him.

COMMUNICATION

As in any other relationship, we need to communicate with the person we're in a relationship with, or else there isn't much of a connection. It would be pretty difficult to have a best friend you never talked to. Perhaps you'd think a lot about them and have pleasant memories of things you've done together, but it takes ongoing communication to maintain a relationship and deepen the friendship.

You didn't fall in love with your spouse by staring out the window in silence on every date, right? At one point or another, the conversations and time spent together sparked an irresistible urge to be near each other. Remember those phone conversations that lasted for hours and the long walks that made time seem to stand still? You were connecting with each other in thought, word, and deed. Eventually everything became about your love. You couldn't get him or her off your mind, and every moment you spent apart felt as if something was missing. Remember that?

Then came marriage and maybe even kids, and then the work of the relationship settled over you. You discovered that maintaining the connection takes effort and commitment and the willingness to set aside preferences to stay focused on moving in the same direction. This is the anatomy of relationships. It's beautiful and messy and serendipitous and difficult and transcendent. And that was just Tuesday. It's life *with* the one you love, and the togetherness is worth the effort because it's making you stronger and wiser and more whole.

A basic building block for any relationship moving forward is good communication. But for some reason, we often put our relationship with God in a different category.

Have you ever listened to people talk to God? Have you ever listened to yourself talk to Him? We would never talk to anyone else the way we often talk to God. Imagine calling from the living room to your spouse in the kitchen like this: "I beseech thee, flesh of my flesh—wouldst thou in thy kindness hearken unto my voice and provide for thine partner bread from the grain of the fields and lettuce from the orchard, and wouldst thou with thine own hands form a sandwich and bring it unto me?"

I realize I'm exaggerating a little, but I've heard people talk to God like this all my life. Why do we think our relationship with Him would work any other way than what is natural to us? Do we think God is looking for something completely foreign?

What God Is Looking For

What God wants is an honest, loving, loyal, and intimate relationship with us. We often put Him in a completely different category and only talk to Him when we're facing difficulties or offering words of gratitude or songs of worship. Oh, and thanks for our meals, of course. These are completely appropriate, but what God wants is to be *with* us—to be the first and most important love of our lives (Revelation 2:4-5) because this is the place we hold in His heart.

Have you ever been in love with someone who constantly kept you at an emotional arm's length? It was torture, wasn't it? Why would we do this to the One who gave us the gift of life and proves His unstoppable love for us continually? We're not going to find truer love anywhere. It's not possible to find something deeper or more committed. This is what we're searching for. When we seek for what only God can fill in another relationship, not only will we get crushed, but we also are centering our identity in something that will certainly fail.

Think about lost loves. Think about the past mistakes

you've made in relationships. Consider the way you've been flattened because you hoped with all your heart in something that did not work in the end. Think of the ways you've tried to carry an emotional load on behalf of someone else and ended up exhausted and alone. Without a core relationship with God that is authentic, natural, collaborative, and non-compartmentalized, we will never find the richness of a properly ordered relationship with anyone else. And as we've talked about before, far too often this is what we're expecting of God in the relationship—that He do all the giving and we do the receiving.

Prayer Life or Life Prayer

God wants to be our first love because we are His. We were made for this. In Him we live and move and have our being (Acts 17:28), and it doesn't require all sorts of mystery and magic. It requires that we give our hearts completely and naturally, as we would to anyone we love and trust. We can't just have a "prayer life" distinct from the rest of our lives. It's almost an oxymoron. God doesn't want us to just set aside some of our time out of guilt or obligation so that we can fulfill our duty and talk to Him. How would that work in your other relationships? This is like saying, if you're married, that you have a "spouse life" distinct from the rest of your life—a segregated part of life that isn't holistic and integrated. If the time you spend and the intimacy you share with your spouse is based on guilt, duty, or obligation, what sort of relationship do you have? Not a particularly life-giving and nourishing one.

God isn't interested in being an obligation. He wants to be our everything. He wants to be holistically included in everything we do and think and dream about and hope for. He wants to enter into the doubt, fear, joy, and pain with us. He doesn't want to be a segmented part of our lives. He wants to *be* our lives. He is our very source of life (John 7:37-39). We must reframe our picture of what interacting with God is all about. He's not there just for crises. Talking to Him isn't just about gratefulness or worship or petition or complaint. It's all of that and everything else that happens every day.

Let's do a little exercise to locate the spiritual compartment we often try to keep God in. What wouldn't you do if you believed God was present? Think about that for a minute. There are things we wouldn't do if we had openly invited God to be with us everywhere we go, in every conversation we have, in every action we take, and inside every decision we make. Inviting God to be *with* us in everything will connect us constantly to things that give life and keep us from what will steal it away.

If we're inviting God into everything that we do, think, and say, then *life itself becomes a prayer*. Talking to God and simply being present to Him becomes the great adventure of life and not just a compartmentalized duty. If we are allowing His presence into all our activities and secret thoughts and aspirations, then He is involved in who we are and who we are becoming. He is nourishing us with His life and inviting us forward through the conversational intimacy we share every day in relationship.

When life itself has become a prayer, we are connected to that source of love and life. This is the nourishment we need and desperately crave. This is the nourishment we've been scratching and clawing at life to find. This insatiable hunger for life that has been consuming us can actually be fed.

Understanding that life itself can be a prayer takes the guilt of not praying enough completely out of the equation because we're constantly interacting with God. It makes a world of difference to be intimately and constantly connected to the Creator of life itself (Genesis 1:27; 1 John 5:20.)

It's not about a time clock that you have to punch to make sure you're giving enough minutes to God. In life, if there is a stopwatch for the amount of time you get to talk or listen, then you're typically paying for that time with a therapist or consultant or attorney. It's a transaction, not a relationship. Good conversation just happens. Conversational intimacy happens in the spoken places, and it happens in the silent spaces between. A relationship is always happening. Invite God into every act and aspect of your life at all times and in all places. To be oriented to God through the Bible, involved in an ongoing conversation with Him that never ceases, is the rich spiritual nourishment we need in order to thrive as we were meant to.

DOES GOD UNDERSTAND?

I realize there are abusive relationships. I understand that for some, the idea of giving your heart to God or anyone else is difficult because of what you've been through. Perhaps you've been deeply betrayed or have been verbally or physically abused. Perhaps parts of your heart are truly broken to the idea of a relationship that is conversational and nourishing—even a relationship with God. Maybe you haven't been able to get past "why?" when you talk to God. You can't seem to go deeper because your heart is broken, and you just can't take the chance of being let down again.

If this is you, I am so sorry this happened to you. I sincerely am. But I want you to know that God didn't do it. I don't want to trivialize anything you've experienced. I want to honor you in it. But so does God. He didn't do that to you, and you have to release Him from that assumption. You have to fight for your life to get it back. The evil one broke you while spinning the blame onto the only one who can heal your broken heart (Psalm 147:3; Isaiah 61:1; Luke 4:18).

Would it surprise you that God knows exactly what it feels like to be betrayed and abused? Throughout the Scriptures we see God not only begging His children to remain true and warning them of the unwanted destiny they were creating for themselves, but also revealing what their wandering and rejection did to His heart. The descriptions in Ezekiel 16 and Hosea 2 are riveting and heartbreaking. God's heart is so invested in a relationship that He uses imagery only a deeply betrayed lover could truly understand.

> On the day you were born your cord was not cut,
> nor were you washed with water to make you clean,
> nor were you rubbed with salt or wrapped in cloths.
> No one looked on you with pity or had compassion
> enough to do any of these things for you. Rather,
> you were thrown out into the open field, for on the
> day you were born you were despised.

Then I passed by and saw you kicking about in your blood, and as you lay there in your blood I said to you, "Live!" I made you grow like a plant of the field. You grew and developed and entered puberty. Your breasts had formed and your hair had grown, yet you were stark naked.

Later I passed by, and when I looked at you and saw that you were old enough for love, I spread the corner of my garment over you and covered your naked body. I gave you my solemn oath and entered into a covenant with you, declares the Sovereign LORD, and you became mine.

I bathed you with water and washed the blood from you and put ointments on you. I clothed you with an embroidered dress and put sandals of fine leather on you. I dressed you in fine linen and covered you with costly garments. I adorned you with jewelry: I put bracelets on your arms and a necklace around your neck, and I put a ring on your nose, earrings on your ears and a beautiful crown on your head. So you were adorned with gold and silver; your clothes were of fine linen and costly fabric and embroidered cloth. Your food was honey, olive oil and the finest flour. You became very beautiful and rose to be a queen. And your fame spread among the nations on account of your beauty, because the splendor I had given you made your beauty perfect, declares the Sovereign LORD.

But you trusted in your beauty and used your fame to become a prostitute. You lavished your favors on anyone who passed by and your beauty became his. You took some of your garments to make gaudy high places, where you carried on your prostitution. You went to him, and he possessed your beauty. You also took the fine jewelry I gave you, the jewelry made of my gold and silver, and you made for yourself male idols and engaged in prostitution with them. And you took your embroidered clothes to put on them, and you offered my oil and incense before them. Also the food I provided for you—the flour, olive oil and honey I gave you to eat—you offered as fragrant incense before them. That is what happened, declares the Sovereign LORD.

And you took your sons and daughters whom you bore to me and sacrificed them as food to the idols. Was your prostitution not enough? You slaughtered my children and sacrificed them to the idols. In all your detestable practices and your prostitution you did not remember the days

of your youth, when you were naked and bare,
kicking about in your blood.

EZEKIEL 16:4-22

Apparently God does know what it feels like to be
betrayed. This sense of loss can only happen when a heart
is invested fully into a relationship. God loves us so profoundly that our rejection, misunderstanding, and mis-
characterization hurts deeply. But God has never been
willing to surrender us. We can reject Him, but He will
not give up the fight for our hearts. This is stunning and
humbling. Where we would turn to rage and bitterness
because of betrayal and abuse He always moves toward
redemption and restoration.

"But then I will win her back once again. I will
lead her into the desert and speak tenderly to
her there. I will return her vineyards to her and
transform the Valley of Trouble into a gateway
of hope. She will give herself to me there, as she
did long ago when she was young, when I freed
her from her captivity in Egypt. When that day
comes," says the LORD, "you will call me 'my
husband' instead of 'my master.'"

HOSEA 2:14-16, NLT

God's love is unspeakably beautiful. It is impossible to understand the depth of His patience and forgiveness. His love is vast and far beyond our own capability, and it's available. It's all about you and all about what you do next.

START HERE

I realize there are many kinds of prayer. I'm not attempting to oversimplify prayer any more than I was trying to oversimplify the Bible. But here's how it is: If we don't have a conversational relationship with God, all we do when we enter into other forms of prayer is bark orders at God and throw His promises at Him, thinking we have the authority to boss Him around and make Him move. It's a completely different thing to walk with God and first invite Him into every aspect of what we think and do—before we start asking Him to do things. When we live in His presence and we are oriented to Him through His Word we'll have a pretty good understanding of what He's doing because we're in a relationship with Him. And He will certainly guide us deeper. Deeper in prayer, deeper into the nuances and mysteries of His Word, deeper into how He wants us to intercede or cleanse or heal or battle—even deep enough to invite us into irreversible change.

THE NOURISHMENT OF REFRAMING

God came to be *with* us in Jesus and faced humanity in all its beautiful, smelly, confused mess. He lived among us, growing and experiencing everything that we do (Hebrews 4:15). And in the end we find Him with tears streaming down His face because He's speaking truth into humanity, not through prophets or miraculous signs in the heavens (Matthew 23:37) but in human flesh—and still we rejected Him.

Jesus was a sinless, perfect person who was betrayed by a friend and mercilessly abused physically and emotionally before being executed in a humiliating and ghastly way. This is God we're talking about here. Make no mistake: God understands the hardships of loving someone who does not love back, and He knows the pain of abuse and rejection firsthand—yet still He came for us. And He still comes for you. He will not surrender you. God most certainly understands the work involved in a relationship.

If we could just glimpse the depth of love we're talking about here, it would profoundly reframe God in our minds and hearts. He wants a relationship with you so badly that He's willing to die for it. He understands you so profoundly that He left infinity and entered time and space and every sad thing that humanity could throw at

Him to identify with you in person and then offer the rescue of your very soul. He came to reclaim your identity. To give you back to yourself.

Want to be nourished?

Reframe your spiritual life. Everything is spiritual.

Reframe the Bible. It is a friend, not a bully.

Reframe your prayer life. Life is a prayer.

Reframe God. He is not aloof and distant. He has done everything you allow Him to do in order to be *with* you.

Notes

1. Cornelius Plantinga, *Not the Way It's Supposed to Be: A Breviary of Sin* (Grand Rapids, MI: Eerdmans, 1995), 10.

PART THREE
RESTART

*We must be willing to get rid of the life we've planned,
so as to have the life that is waiting for us. The old skin has
to be shed before the new one can come.*

JOSEPH CAMPBELL,
THE HERO'S JOURNEY

*Although no one can go back and make a brand new start,
anyone can start from now and make a brand new ending.*

CARL BARD

A Sunrise is God's way of saying, "Let's start again."

TODD STOCKER

Chapter 6

RESTARTING CHANGE

*Time heals griefs and quarrels, for we change and
are no longer the same persons. Neither the offender
nor the offended are any more themselves.*
BLAISE PASCAL

*You will suddenly realize that the reason you never
changed before was because you didn't want to.*
ROBERT SCHULLER,
REACH OUT FOR NEW LIFE

WHOLE

So here we are, the hard part: change. Nobody likes it much. Shifting away from what is familiar in exchange for the work of reorienting our lives in a new way is hard, and it exposes just how deep the ruts in our lives are sometimes. Look at how hard it is to keep those New Year's resolutions!

The work of change in our lives is a necessary part of growth, but changing our relationship with God feels a little dodgy, doesn't it? We have a sort of "permanency complex" with Him—like nothing is supposed to ever change. This is borne out of our fear of getting something wrong, of believing the wrong thing and heading down the wrong spiritual path. So we stay with the pack. We listen to all the hearsay and build the model and gather the data. We follow back through the loop we've always been on when God has always been inviting us into a personal relationship—not a group friendship. Don't get me wrong. Living in community and walking through life together with other believers is critical. This is absolutely heralded in Scripture and forms the body of Christ in the world. Our friends and allies are irreplaceable in our faith journey in every conceivable way. But they're not a replacement for a personal relationship with God. You can't have a "group marriage." That would be . . . weird. In the same way, you can't have a group relationship with God.

On the day that you go before the heavenly Father and offer an account of your life, you won't be able to drag anyone else with you to blame. God is inviting you into a first-person, collaborative relationship with Him. Replacing this with anything less is how things stay shallow. The relationship can't go deep enough to penetrate our hearts and change us irreversibly. We want to experience spiritual growth, but we don't always have the life-or-death urgency we would if, for example, our house was on fire.

That might need to change.

After all, this whole thing is all about you—this beautiful, extravagant, decadent, over-generous life that's been given as a gift—and it's all about what you do next.

In John's Gospel, Jesus visited a giant pool structure known as Bethesda. Its ruins remain to this day in Jerusalem. While there he had an encounter with a man who had been disabled for thirty-eight years. Rather than just healing the man, He asked him a question. "Do you want to be made whole?"

This is really the question of just about every change we contemplate in our lives.

If you want the life-giving and collaborative relationship with God we've been contemplating in this book, perhaps Jesus is asking you the same question: Do you want to be made whole? Do you want *shalom* in your life? If so, it's probably going to require the work of change, and when it comes to our faith we don't usually like to consider deconstructing it so that something new can come bursting out.

So why do we resist change so fiercely? Is an unchanging life even possible? Let's spend a few minutes examining what change is and where it can lead us in our relationship with God.

OUR CHANGE

After the birth of our son Maxwell, my wife, Jill, had a case of postpartum blues. Although this is fairly common, the blues grew until she began to slip into the blackness of depression. There were no apparent reasons for her to feel depressed or overwhelmed, but the depression became an all-consuming monster. We kept thinking it would wear off. We resisted exploring its origins, thinking it would simply go away eventually.

I'll never forget the crushing call that came a couple of years into the battle when my previously vibrant wife told me she was so overwhelmed that she had hit bottom and didn't know what she might do.

It was obvious that change was needed, but we didn't know where to turn. We tweaked our lifestyle, trying to find the right balance rather than diving headlong into any deep change. Fear of the unknown kept us neutralized.

The thought of seeing a doctor for antidepressant medication was something Jill fought hard against. When she finally conceded, the medication seemed to take the edge off for a while but left her miserably numb. Eventually the medicine didn't work anymore. Hopelessness returned with a fury.

Jill began a several-year cycle of displaying two different

personalities—the wife I'd married and a very angry someone else. Our marriage began to feel like a minefield. It felt as if we were losing everything we had dreamed of. What should have brought us the most joy brought only pain and confusion.

On good days we'd talk about it. It was very difficult for Jill to understand the extreme ways in which she was behaving. It was even more difficult to acknowledge that mental illness might be involved. The fear of this diagnosis was paralyzing to her. Even in the blackness of depression, with hope nothing more than a distant memory, it still seemed that to change course and find a biological root in her mind would be worse.

As this decade-long battle continued to worsen, Jill finally made the difficult choice to see a psychiatrist. Unfortunately, there was little help to be found. We had finally become desperate enough to acknowledge something was severely wrong only to find that mental illness was not the problem either. Throughout this process Jill felt hopeless that she would ever have a normal life again. She was fearful of what might become of her and desperate for answers. Nothing in any field of science or faith was making any sense.

Finally, as we began to resign ourselves to living in what felt like the realm of insanity, Jill found a doctor who diagnosed a mutant gene that runs in her family line. This gene disallows the body from absorbing many essential vitamins and minerals and had shut down her thyroid almost completely. The symptoms that accompany this condition were chillingly familiar. Within the month after the diagnosis and resultant treatment, Jill's equilibrium began to return. Within a couple of months, the light began to come on inside her, and several years later she has her life—body, mind, soul, and spirit—back.

The irony is that years passed between these steps. We fought change at every turn. We feared the unknown more than the hardship of what we knew, and although this is our story, almost any story could be overlaid on this one. We fight change with a vengeance even though it is the normal and constant way of life.

Change is necessary. There are necessary beginnings and necessary endings throughout our lives, and to deny this and fight change is to refuse to grow forward. This unfortunately leads to stagnation. We typically don't embrace change because we're afraid of it. Fear of the unknown drives us into a box that we think we can control and manage. This is unhealthy, not to mention impossible. Fear is not from God (2 Timothy 1:7). Fear leads back through the loop of assumptions you've played in your life: *You are ultimately on your own because God may not come through. You have to be prepared to handle life on your own.*

WHY FEAR CHANGE?

The fear of change has more to do with us than with God not being there for us. The stories of our lives are full of missteps and failures. And we don't want to repeat those things. They hurt us, so we put "road closed" signs up on those pathways where we failed. But were the roads wrong, or was it the fact that we took our eyes off the road and ended up in the ditch? All our "road closed" signs leave us with nowhere else to go. We're trapped in a cage, too fearful to move.

Your destiny may actually be down a road that you've closed off completely. God may be pulling you toward a place where you've failed in the past, and going down that road may require that you set aside the barriers you've placed at the on-ramp. But you'll have to be willing to change if you ever hope to get there.

Remember the assumptions we talked about in chapter 2? Leaping to conclusions or filling in gaps to create a seamless, logical reality, even though it might be completely incorrect? This isn't something we do only to others or to God. We do this to ourselves, too. We make assumptions about who we are based mostly on failures and wounds, and we can arrive at pictures of ourselves that are totally incorrect. As we reframe our relationships with God, we're also going to have to be willing to reframe ourselves, which can be the most difficult part of the process. But what is a reframe if it's not change?

You are not who you once were. Everything about you has been constantly changing. To define yourself by your past regrets or mistakes is to deny the power of God to redeem you and deny your God-given ability to grow and mature. When you are afraid of where you are going because of the injuries of where you have been, it is a very lonely place. But when you are living in this present, ever-changing moment, you will realize God is right here *with* you, as He has always been. We have to get comfortable with change. We have to embrace it fully because God is constantly on the move.

CONSTANCY AND CHANGE

We rely on the permanence of the earth, don't we? It's our home. If it falls apart, we have no place to go, so we depend on its relatively unchanging nature. Did you know that the stability of the earth is an illusion? There are seven major plates that make up the earth's uppermost mantle or crust. Then there are seven smaller ones and many, many more tertiary or subplates.[1] These make up the ground we walk on, drive on, build our houses on, and depend on to grow our food; to provide pathways for our water supply; and to support our lives. When these plates suddenly slip on a fault, the earth quakes. It shifts and can shake up everything around it for hundreds of miles.[2] It's estimated that these quakes—ranging from small and unnoticeable to large and destructive—happen about four thousand times a day.[3] The earth that we rely on to be constant is actually constantly unstable and in a state of change.

Let's get closer to home. Your body is changing every second of every single day. Did you know that the outer layer of your skin completely replaces itself about every two weeks? The most visible part of you is constantly and rapidly changing, and there's nothing you can do about it. Even in death you can't stop the constant changing of your physical form. Your entire body is continually cycling. Every seven years to ten years, almost every cell that makes up who you are is replaced. Skin tissue, muscles, blood cells, spinal cord, lungs, liver, taste buds, vocal cords, kneecaps—everything gets completely replaced.[4] You are literally not who you were a few years ago. Every single cell has been replaced.

Change is inevitable. The economy changes, weather patterns change, political powers change, relationships change, seasons change, music changes, technology changes, clothing changes, transportation changes. There are changes to our health, our family size, the restaurants we like to frequent, the size of the city we live in. One hundred years ago women were fighting for the right to vote; now the Internet connects the world in real time and fuels revolutions. Rapid change has been going on for millennia. We are not the people we once were. It's fascinating that we aim for what is constant when all we ever do is constantly change. The only thing that seems to remain truly constant about us is that at our core we are created in the image of God—and for some reason He wants to be *with us* in all our changes.

INVITED TO CHANGE

When we are tempted to avoid change in our faith, we have to recognize that God is in it. We have to reframe one of the most fascinating things about God: He is constantly inviting us to change. We never get to settle in. When we are tired and just want to lie down and forget the whole thing, He is like a good physical trainer saying, "You can do five more. You can do it."

God knows what spiritual stagnation will bring to our lives and that nothing good can come from it. The Scriptures show us the depth of this truth in vivid high-definition. God will not allow us to create our own personal heavens. And we pursue control and comfort more than we probably realize in an attempt to craft it. But it's all trickery. It is an overweight person telling himself, "It's not that bad" or the anorexic looking in the mirror and seeing a normal body. It is the addict saying, "I have this under control" or the starving person losing her hunger pains because her stomach is atrophying.

It is the tempter in the Garden of Eden saying you can be your own god—that you can construct and control a comfortable life, when in reality that comfortable life is no more than a pretty cage. It's the taming of the human spirit that we choose, leaving behind the wild, unfettered creative nature that is hardwired into our DNA by the very image of God in us. The personal heavens we try to craft for ourselves quickly become personal hells that are killing us but we can find no way out so we fill it with more plastic and battery-operated blinking lights to distract us from the truth that we've become like tamed zoo animals when we were born to be free.

We have to embrace the fact that change is an active part of our faith journey—and, yes, some of it will be hard. But it's time, isn't it?

CHANGE IN THE CHRISTIAN LIFE

You've invested some time into considering what a relationship with God isn't and what it could be. You've also considered nourishing your soul. If you follow through with this, it is going to change your faith. And the suggestion of rethinking and reframing faith is something that historically makes us very uneasy. We want something stable and permanent so that there are no unanswered questions about eternity. Being wrong could shake our paradigms and rock us to the core. We don't like to think about our faith as something that should change.

But it's an unhealthy illusion that we can find a life-giving, collaborative relationship with God where He won't ask us to change. He constantly invites us to change. He won't allow us to become comfortable, complacent, and stagnant (Revelation 3:16). He'll always blow apart the cozy boxes or ironclad cages we construct for ourselves— or Him. These are essentially ways of saying we want to be the masters of our own lives—to functionally be our own gods. They bring us back to the forbidden fruit in the Garden of Eden. We are not meant for this. We are made to be *with* God and to live a grand adventure together.

The early Christian church was changing from the moment of its inception. The Good News captured the hearts of thousands, who began to talk about it in traveling caravans and on ships sailing for distant shores. It was carried from person to person across deserts and oceans. As the apostles planted churches, a human organism began to collectively form. We now know this as the body of Christ. But, just as our human bodies are constantly changing, this body has always been changing. Babies are born and people die. People change the cities they live in. Families change where they worship and find community. People's convictions are influenced by the cultures they live in. New people come to the faith. The body of Christ constantly changes because people constantly change.

The very empire that executed Jesus became the vehicle that spread the legitimacy of faith in Him to the whole world, taking it from the underground to the mainstream and then becoming its guardian and protector. As the Good News spread, more and more rules, traditions, and rituals became necessary to explain the purpose of the church, the way people needed to behave, and the way salvation worked. This has been an ever-changing process.

Things became bloated. The more man attempted to fill in the gaps of the unknown and explain every spiritual eventuality, the thicker the rulebook got. As early as the fourteenth century, people like John Wycliffe were speaking out against the status quo. In 1517 Martin Luther nailed his ninety-five theses to the door of All Saints' Church in Wittenberg, Saxony, and sparked the Protestant Reformation. This was a fundamental and momentous shift in the story of the Christian faith. It was a colossal shift of spiritual tectonic plates. The ensuing spiritual earthquake was so staggering and far-reaching that its aftershocks are still being felt more than five hundred years later.

Because of the Reformation it is estimated that the world is now home to 41,000 Christian denominations.[5] The body of Christ has branched into many styles, shapes, sizes, streams, and nuances. And we're all constantly growing. We're all undergoing the process of change.

You've probably experienced some of this kind of change many times in your own life—change that has, believe it or not, *changed* your faith. Haven't you had those moments when something clicks into place and you experience an awareness or a revelation of something that unlocks truth inside you—an understanding about God that you never had before? Sometimes these are small tremors or *aha* moments, and sometimes the tectonic plates of our lives shift dramatically, expanding truths and shaking off old assumptions. This is what I hope is happening as we reframe our relationship to and with God together—a shift colossal enough to move you dramatically and irreversibly forward.

The Changing of Your Faith

Your faith wasn't downloaded in its entirety on the day you believed. Your understanding of God, His work in the world, and His work inside you happen with time. Your understanding increases because of the big and small changes that happen every single day. You grow because you change. Your faith expands and contracts like the living, changing thing it is. We are all a part of this process of transformation. This is *sanctification*—the step-by-step, day-by-day process of being made holy and set apart to God[6] (John 17:17; Acts 26:18; Romans 6:1-23; 2 Corinthians 5:17; Galatians 2:20; Ephesians 4:13; Philippians 1:6; 1 Thessalonians 5:23; 2 Thessalonians 2:13; 2 Timothy 2:21; Hebrews 9:14; 10:14; 13:21; 2 Peter 1:2-4; 3:18; Jude 1:24).

When you first believed the Good News that Jesus died for you, you had an awakening inside, and you've continued to wake up ever since. The process of sanctification by default requires the active agent of change over time. We are completely different people from when we started. And we must not fight against this but embrace it if we want freedom. The Greek word μετανοέω (*metanoeó*) is something Scripture repeatedly invites us to do: *Repent*. And this active and necessary word means to *change* your mind or to *change* your inner person.[7] In other words, it means to *reframe* the way you've been looking at things and choose something different.

More often than not we think of change with negative

baggage attached to it. Change means that something old is being replaced by something new, and for some reason we don't like to let go of the old. It feels like a sort of failure. But nothing new can begin unless something else is ending. We need to completely reframe change and embrace it as a constant and never-ending part of our faith journey or we will find ourselves stuck. And while we fight to keep things the same we will unintentionally strangle the faith we have, leaving us with something lifeless that no longer inspires and no longer matters.

The Changing of the Bible

We also need to acknowledge that even the Bible has changed over time. This is a simple fact of history. I love the Word of God with all my heart, and I believe it completely because I've seen its effect on my life and in the lives of tens of thousands of people. I believe it is the compass that orients us to God's heart. But it has changed over time. At first it was out of simple inevitability. It hadn't all been inspired yet. Then it was shaped over the course of Jewish history out of necessity.

When the children of Israel were in exile, they could no longer be people of the temple. The destruction of the temple, which had become their identity, forced them to find new ways to remember who they were. To shape their faith within the new culture they were assimilated into, they became people of the Scriptures. The Scriptures weren't centered around a location. They were portable, flexible, and indestructible.[8] God sent prophets to be His mouthpieces, but often it wasn't until much later that the people realized God had inspired what was being heralded and it was something to be revered and held sacred.

The Scriptures Jesus had were not identical to the Scriptures King David had. Much more had been revealed. By the time Jesus came, King David's poetry and songs had been collected and recognized as a holy gift inspired by God. The Bible we have is not what Jesus had either. Jesus didn't have the New Testament. The accounts of Jesus' life and the writings of the apostles hadn't been gathered yet. The early believers knew they had accounts of Jesus' life and sayings and letters written by men who had walked with Jesus and by church fathers like the apostle Paul, but there were all kinds of things floating around about why Jesus had come and what His life meant.

During the first century and a half after Jesus departed, the early church began to take form, and certain writings began to carry significant weight—more than just a recollection or a set of ethics and rules. By AD 200, twenty-one of the accounts and letters had been recognized as inspired writings. It wasn't until the late fourth century that all twenty-seven New Testament books were solidified and officially considered holy Scripture by Christians.[9]

My point here is not to cast doubt on the holy Scriptures or on the church. I would never do that. It would be like putting a pistol to the head of my faith and pulling the trigger. The point isn't doubt. The point is that change is constantly occurring and has always been around. Believing that we can simply search for and acquire the bedrock of our own devices is an illusion. Everything changes. Nothing that is alive can remain alive without change. And the Word of God is alive (Hebrews 4:12). We have to rethink and reframe what permanence and change mean and embrace something that has always been happening anyway.

We simply don't know all we think we know. But God does. And He wants to be in an intimate, collaborative, and life-giving relationship with us. He doesn't want to be encased in the cement of our every tradition. He wants to be *with* us in the moment we call now. And with every moment there is change.

CHOOSING

Opening your heart completely and granting full and unimpeded access to God with no secret closets and no dusty attics will change you and your faith completely because what you think you know isn't all there is. What you thought was dogmatically cemented in place may crumble. What you've heard through hearsay may not be correct. All of the facts you thought were so ironclad may not add up. All of the ways you've been using God may not work. Inviting God to be a part of every thought, word, and deed in your life and giving Him permission to be a part of every action you take will bring profound change. You will be entering into a first-person, always-on, never-off relationship with the God of all at all times and in all places for the rest of eternity.

We're talking about the same kind of constant, pervasive, inclusive, confrontational, transcendent, blissful, hopeful, struggling, powerful, all-consuming commitment it takes to be in a successful marriage. And if you are married you understand that it changes you fundamentally and for the rest of your life. Opening our lives completely to a collaborative relationship with God can and will go deeper than that.

But do you want to be made whole?

As we began our journey I recounted a conversation I had with a man who needed to encourage a friend toward dietary change. His friend will probably die if he doesn't change his diet. Think about it. Perhaps this is where you find yourself. Maybe the inner life you've been experiencing is truly starving for more. Maybe a complete reframing of God and your relationship with Him is upon you. Perhaps giving the Scriptures the place of a best friend and counselor and living your life as a prayer has finally clicked the missing pieces in place. Maybe making the necessary adjustments to these realities is the hopeful and difficult work before you.

NO MORE PRETENDING

If you've been in the process of reframing, you've been contemplating change this whole time. But you won't have to do it alone. The God who fiercely loves you is very present. He is *with* you. Being *with you* is all He's ever wanted. But God is not interested in just being our buddy. He certainly does want a friendship with us (John 15:13-15), but this is our Creator we're talking about. He's far too invested in us to be satisfied with a casual acquaintance. He wants us to give Him our broken hearts so that He can give us back whole hearts. He wants us to be everything He created us to be. This will require change.

He'll take us places we've never dreamed of and show us things that will blow our minds. And He'll also begin to pry our fingers off the control we think we have over our lives. He'll invite us to lose ourselves in Him and also to do some difficult things. He'll invite us to surrender what has sabotaged the relationship in the past.

Some of the battles may be difficult because we've probably created identities that need to be dismantled. It's remarkable, the noise a thing makes when it has to die. But for God to do something new inside us, we have to allow what is old and often deep to be replaced—even in our faith. This can be hard work. But be encouraged. Change is something we're doing all the time anyway, and the change we're talking about is what will finally set us free.

Rethink what you know about God. Reframe what you've been calling your relationship with Him. Give the Scriptures the place of a trusted friend. Embrace change. This will restart a relationship with God and begin a new life you never thought possible.

Notes

1. S. K. Haldar, *Introduction to Mineralogy and Petrology* (Waltham, MA: Elsevier, 2013), 89.
2. "Earthquakes, Plate Tectonics, Earth Structure," United States Geological Survey, http://www.usgs.gov/faq/categories/9827/3343 (accessed February 23, 2015).
3. "Earthquake Facts and Statistics," United States Geological Survey, http://earthquake.usgs.gov/earthquakes/eqarchives/year/eqstats.php (accessed February 23, 2015).
4. Nicholas Wade, "Your Body Is Younger Than You Think," *New York Times*, August 2, 2005, http://www.nytimes.com/2005/08/02/science/02cell .html?pagewanted=all&_r=0.
5. "Global Christianity—A Report on the Size and Distribution of the

World's Christian Population: Appendix B," Pew Research Center, December 19, 2011, 95; http://www.pewforum.org/2011/12/19 /global-christianity-exec/.

6. M. G. Easton, *Illustrated Bible Dictionary*, third edition, s.v. "sanctification."

7. M. G. Easton, *Illustrated Bible Dictionary*, third edition, s.v. "repentance."

8. *Ashbury Bible Commentary: Part 1: General Articles*, "Canon of Scripture," https://www.biblegateway.com/resources/asbury-bible-commentary /Canon-Scripture.

9. Ibid.

Chapter 7

RESTARTING EVERYTHING

Your heart and my heart are very, very old friends.

HAFIZ,
"YOUR MOTHER AND MY MOTHER"

I hope you live a life you're proud of. If you find that you're not,
I hope you have the strength to start all over again.

ERIC ROTH,
THE CURIOUS CASE OF BENJAMIN BUTTON

"Look at that sea, girls—all silver and shadow and vision of
things not seen. We couldn't enjoy its loveliness any more if we had
millions of dollars and ropes of diamonds."

L. M. MONTGOMERY,
ANNE OF GREEN GABLES

EZEKIEL

For a moment we thought we could lose the baby. Nine months had come down to an instant decision. After six hours of excruciating labor our midwife told us something was terribly wrong and we needed to get to the hospital immediately. We'd had a contingency plan in place for months. In the event we would need intervention we'd travel to Nashville to have the baby, but she told us we needed to skip Nashville and get to the nearest hospital at once.

I drove as fast as I dared while listening to my wife's agonizing moans. I raced into the emergency room driveway and piled Jill and her midwife out of the van, and in an instant they were gone. I walked through the door of the emergency room and was immediately whisked to the second floor. Jill appeared to be wired from head to toe. We were told that the baby was under terrible stress, exhausted, and his heart rate was way below normal and dropping. The baby needed immediate surgical intervention, or we risked his life. The sack surrounding his little body had torn, and he was being exposed to all sorts of things he wasn't supposed to be. Jill's body was being wracked by nonstop spasmodic contractions

It all happened so fast. There wasn't time to process. There wasn't time to pray and listen. There wasn't time to contemplate anything. We had one minute to make the choice.

Jill's greatest fear in this pregnancy was an emergency intervention. And now it was imminent and there was nothing I could do about it. It was a helpless feeling.

She looked at me and said through the oxygen mask, "We have to do it. We can't lose him."

As they rolled her away, her hands were clammy and

shaking with fear. We exchanged quivering words of love, not knowing if we were saying good-bye to each other or to our baby.

Five minutes after Jill was wheeled into surgery, Ezekiel was born. Fifteen minutes after our frightened good-bye he was in my arms. Thirty minutes after the instant decision he was at his mother's breast, and he has traveled around the world with us since.

Last week I watched this little boy running on the beach outside of Oceanside, California. His little legs were pumping as fast as he could move them. Watching his wide-eyed fascination with every smooth stone on the beach gave me a rush of exquisite gratitude. But as I stood there alone for a moment, watching my family play along the shore, I had a powerful sense of God's smile along with my own. It was as if He had floated in on the last wave and was standing next to me. I felt His inspiration. For a moment I felt His joy and hope for this baby boy exceeding even my own.

I thought about this later in the evening when Ezekiel finally fell asleep. Certainly I sensed God's hope for who Ezekiel was created to be, but in the moment I felt as if God had hopes and dreams for every person on the beach, and even for every life in the world.

INSPIRING GOD

Would it shock you to find out you inspired God? What kind of weight would this idea bring to your life? *You inspire God.* That would shift a paradigm or two, wouldn't it? It would probably make you think a little longer about living recklessly or, for that matter, not living at all.

If the definition of *inspiration* is something "that makes someone want to do or create something,"[1] then we must inspire God because life is still being created and given as a gift—seven beautiful screaming new lives per second, to be exact. But to inspire is more than that. To *inspire* also means "the action or power of moving the intellect or emotions."[2] The entire narrative of the Bible reveals a God who is eager and willing to be *with* us. In the Old Testament, God was constantly moved to act and respond. The Scriptures are full of stories in which He describes the way our actions affect Him. And then, in the most profound action the world has ever seen, God came in person. Jesus came. If people don't inspire God, then why would He come for us? Why would He care? Why would He want to be *with* us?

We inspire God. This final reframe should touch just about everything in our lives, leaving them humbled and tingling with possibility. As I've said so many times before, this really is all about you, and all about what you do next.

My friend, you were created and fashioned after God's

image. Do you understand how profoundly you matter? Do you understand how profoundly *that* matters? If God's image is embedded in you at your spiritual core and God gave you the breath of life (Genesis 2:7), then He is more deeply invested in you than every single one of the cells that give you form and shape. You cannot escape God. And He will not abandon you.

INTERTWINED INSPIRATION

In his first letter, the apostle John described it like this:

> No one has ever seen God; but if we love one another, God lives *in us* and his love is made complete in us.
>
> This is how we know that we live *in him* and he *in us*: He has given us of his Spirit. And we have seen and testify that the Father has sent his Son to be the Savior of the world. If anyone acknowledges that Jesus is the Son of God, God lives *in them* and they *in God*. And so we know and rely on the love God has for us.
>
> God is love. Whoever lives in love lives *in God*, and God *in them*.
>
> I JOHN 4:12-16, EMPHASIS ADDED

This isn't a rogue Scripture verse taken out of context. From His own lips Jesus said, "I have given them the glory that you gave me, that they may be one as we are one—*I in them* and you in me—so that they may be brought to complete unity. Then the world will know that you sent me and have loved them even as you have loved me" (John 17:22-23, emphasis added).

Or perhaps we should go to one of the most popular Scriptures of all time: "I have been crucified with Christ and I no longer live, but Christ lives *in me*. The life I now live in the body, I live by faith in the Son of God, who loved me and gave himself for me" (Galatians 2:20, emphasis added). Or this oft-quoted passage: "You, dear children, are from God and have overcome them, because the one who is *in you* is greater than the one who is in the world" (1 John 4:4, emphasis added).

We could keep going—just look at John 14:19-20; John 15:3-5; Romans 8:9; 2 Corinthians 4:8-11; 2 Corinthians 13:5; Galatians 4:19; Ephesians 3:14-17; Colossians 1:27; Colossians 3:9-11; and 1 John 3:24.

We inspire God so much that He wants to be near us, for us, about us, around us, protecting us, nurturing us, saving us, living inside us, and in every other way *with* us. God loves us—very much. We inspire Him and He inspires us.

Doesn't this inspire you to awe?

We matter to God so deeply that our whole lives should hum with His presence. None of the things that have been incapacitating us should hold anywhere near the persistent weight they have had in the past. Do they even matter? How much of what we obsess about actually matters in the face of the Almighty God's profound love for us and the offer of a life-giving, collaborative relationship with Him? This changes everything. What can we do but fall to our knees and cry, "Holy, holy, holy is the Lord God Almighty, who was, and is, and is to come" (Revelation 4:8)?

It's breathtaking.

The apostle Paul wrote, "All these promises are made to us, my dear friends. So then, let us purify ourselves from everything that makes body or soul unclean, and let us be completely holy by living in awe of God" (2 Corinthians 7:1, GNT).

Knowing that you inspire God, and being inspired by Him in return, should make you want to restart a new life *with* God. And all of this is available. If we will allow this reframe to change us irreversibly and enter into a moment-by-moment collaboration with Him, we can restart something profoundly beautiful. God has been waiting for this. He's been waiting a long time to be more than a compartment in your life. When He created you He dreamed of this, and the hunger inside you has been pulling you back toward Him so that your life can be lived inspired by the One who authored it. So why do we need to reframe, and what happens when we do?

THE REFRAMED LIFE

Coming Home

Return to Me. This has been God's constant plea. *Come back to Me, accept Me, receive Me, believe Me, come to Me, trust Me.* I could fill pages with Bible references to show how pervasive and persistent this theme is. God wants you *with* Him. You are a masterpiece to Him. You inspire Him, and He cannot stand to see you living as anything less than His beloved while you misunderstand His heart and blame Him for things that He hasn't done. The ill-placed assumptions from the wounds in your life and the spin of the evil one trying to convince you that his thievery is actually something God is involved with have estranged you and kept you from giving yourself back to Him completely.

This is your chance. This moment is your reset button. You can restart a completely new relationship with God *right now*. There doesn't need to be fanfare. The sun doesn't need to beam through the window. A breeze doesn't need to appear from out of nowhere. You just have to peel back the picture you've had of God from the old, tired frame you've kept Him in and set Him free in your life. Let Him be who He is inside you so that you can be who you are.

If you'll let the old frame fall to the floor of your life and let God out of the tired box you've stored Him in, you'll notice a rapid shift in orientation. All of a sudden you will have a true north. Your story will no longer be about simply getting out of here. This is how we live a lot of the time isn't it? We can't negotiate the maze of life on our own. It starts feeling like a cage. The only hope we have going forward is to get out of here so that we can be with God and be free of all the confusion. But this is what God has been trying to give us all along—right here, right now. We want to get out of here so that we can be *with* God, but we can be *with* Him right now. This is what God tells us all throughout the Scriptures. In and out of cultural changes and throughout thousands of years He's been begging for our return so that we might find the life we were created to live and stay connected to that source.

I don't want to close my eyes in death and finally see Jesus only to say, "It's so nice to meet You. I've heard so much about You." I want to know Him because our lives have been intertwined for decades. We don't have to wait to start this relationship. The relationship is now. Here.

Our entire story is about moving back to God—returning to Him. And in the process we are moving away from what has held us in bondage for millennia. We are moving away from the spin the evil one has put on our story. We're moving away from the lie that we can be our own gods. We're moving back to innocence (Matthew 18:3). We're going back to the place where the knowledge of good and evil no longer matter to us because God has consumed us wholly—back to the place that He is in us and we are in Him and we're ruined for anything less because we've tasted Eden and nothing can compare. Then in death we will close our eyes to this world and open them to what is next—not an unknown but a truly known.

What Reframing Means

It is critical for this reframing and restarting that you understand a true relationship involves knowing and being known. It's not a one-sided thing. You can't successfully maintain a healthy relationship in which one party is giving all he's got and the other one is taking while giving little back. You've probably been in friendships or relationships like this and know they don't work. Our relationship with God doesn't work any differently. The stakes are just higher.

We often find ourselves in worship environments in

which we're affirming our great desire to know more of God. We'll even sing it: "I want to know you, I want to see your face, I want to know You more." And there is nothing wrong with that. A desire for more of God is something we desperately need, but what about God knowing us? Do you want Him to know *you* more? Because this can't be a lopsided relationship where we're all take and He is all give. That's not a healthy relationship. I realize we could just assume that God is all-knowing and already knows everything about us, but are we actually offering ourselves to Him?

God has given Himself completely. What more could He do to prove His love? What other hoop would we have Him jump through so that we can finally believe He truly loves us and wants to be *with* us? He has devoted Himself to relationship *with* us. How can we give any less? Why should God expect any less?

We can spend our whole lives trying to know God and not be known by Him. We can compartmentalize the relationship, exchange relationship for hearsay, substitute a real connection for data and facts, or use God for what we can get out of the relationship—and in the process not give Him our whole hearts.

This relationship is not just the act of opening your heart to knowing God more fully. It is the act of completely and irreversibly opening your heart to God and giving yourself wholly back to Him—to know *and be known*. It is an all-or-nothing proposition that is before you. It won't work any other way. It won't work any more than a partial marriage would work. If you're not going to give everything you are to this relationship, it's not going to work—now or ever. But if you give everything to your relationship with God, that decision has eternal implications.

Waking Up to Your Legacy

We desperately need to wake up. It's critical that we do. You are a forebearer to hundreds, if not thousands, of people who have yet to be born. I've said many times that this is all about you and all about what you do next, and it is. But what you do next will affect generations of your descendants.

You are here right now breathing oxygen. You have the breath of life within you as a gift from the living God. You are created in His image with a free will and a vast array of choices, but those choices will affect those who are coming behind you. The story found in Scripture has not been concluded. You have the baton in your hand at this moment, but one day it will be passed to a new generation. What you do matters. Everything matters.

What story are you passing on? Is it of a person who

could not wait to get out of here? Is it of someone who lived a very confused life? Or is it the story of a person profoundly ruined for anything but a deep and nourishing relationship with God?

What do you want your legacy to be?

Life can't be just about getting out of here. It's too important. It's too great a gift. We have a vital role to play right here and now. We must. Otherwise the risen Christ could have just set up His kingdom on earth and been done with it. When Jesus returned from the dead, redemption was accomplished. He was already here. Why leave and promise to return at a later date if there weren't more to accomplish?

Jesus built a bridge across the canyon carved by man that separated us from God. From a human perspective, this division was irreversible. We could never make it right and restore ourselves to God. But God would not surrender His beloved children. He came to rescue us. Jesus did what we could not: He restored us to Himself. But we were left here to do what we can—to tell everyone the unspeakably good news that the chasm has been bridged; to steward the extravagant gift of earth, the home He gave us to live on (Genesis 1:28-30); and to bring His kingdom to this world, restoring it to God in collaboration *with*

Him. "Thy kingdom come, Thy will be done *in earth*, as it is in heaven" (Matthew 6:10, KJV; emphasis added).

Counting the Cost

You probably recognize that really entering into a life-giving, collaborative relationship with God is going to irreversibly change you. We've already spent time discussing the fact that we are constantly changing and that to fight change is to refuse to grow up, wake up, and truly live. We've talked about the way an awakened life could look, but I need to be honest about what it will cost.

This world is an extravagant gift—a luxurious home. But broken people live here with us, and broken people are capable of just about anything. Your own story probably bears witness to it. Not everyone is going to wake up. In fact, you may be one of the few who do. Even believers, living out of their brokenness, are capable of terrible things, and some of those actions may touch your life.

I believe God ultimately desires to redeem everyone He created and that restoration is available. I also know that many will not allow it, and God will not usurp a person's will to get to their heart. As humanity learned in the Garden of Eden, love isn't love if there's no way out.

Jesus said, "I have told you all this so that you may have peace in me. Here on earth you will have many trials and sorrows. But take heart, because I have overcome the world" (John 16:33, NLT).

You can't expect that giving your heart completely to God and allowing Him to be *with* you in everything will magically straighten out every wrinkle in everyone else's life on planet Earth. It's a lifelong process. Not everyone is going to go where you're going. Not everyone is going to appreciate the irreversible changes in you, and these changes do not immunize you from interacting with the brokenness of others. You may get hurt. You may get ridiculed. You may even be persecuted. Some relationships may not get repaired. Suffering and hardship will not vanish. It is your orientation to these things that will dramatically shift.

Jesus said, "If the world hates you, keep in mind that it hated me first. If you belonged to the world, it would love you as its own. As it is, you do not belong to the world, but I have chosen you out of the world. That is why the world hates you" (John 15:18-19).

ENLISTED

In coming home, completing this reframing, waking up, and counting the cost, you are enlisting in an epic clash of kingdoms. Once *shalom* ruled, and the peace and order of

God was present in all things. It hasn't been that way here for a long, long time. But that reality will come as those who live within it outnumber those who are unwilling. A kingdom is not overthrown without a fight, and the fight is on. You are engaging in that fight. The first battle is for your heart, and once that is won you have to establish the supply lines to your own nourishment. Then the battle is for your family, friends, neighbors, communities, churches, cities, regions, nations, and the world.

You are engaging in something eternally epic, but you need to know this will cost you everything. If you're holding on to something and that person or item or ambition or goal has more value to you than what God is offering, you need to stop right now and lay it down or walk away. It won't survive the fire of battle—or you won't. This is an all-or-nothing proposition—all that you are in exchange for all that God is. There is no negotiated middle ground. It doesn't work any other way.

A life wholly devoted to God and ruined for anything else is completely worth it. It's almost absurd to say that because the exchange is so heavily lopsided in our favor, but whatever would tether us to anything less will need to be laid down or it will get burned up.

You need to be prepared for some hardship. This isn't magic. It's a relationship with the Almighty God lived out in a broken world that we are here to bring restoration to. It's a valiant and noble cause. Lives that would otherwise be lost will be saved because of your sacrifice along the way. It will be messy at times.

Don't lose faith. Always have hope. *Shalom* is available. God will never, ever abandon you, no matter what you feel. It can't and won't happen. He is woven into the fabric of who you are. He has placed Himself deeper than flesh. He will not leave you, and you will not be forsaken (Deuteronomy 31:6-8; Joshua 1:9; Hebrews 13:5; Revelation 3:10). But there may be hard times along the way.

Even the difficult stretches of road have purpose. We spend so much time trying to avoid suffering in an attempt to make life work, but there's nothing like struggle to loosen our grasp on this world. Jesus' closest friends ended up thinking it was an honor to suffer with Him.

If those times come—and eventually they touch each of us—choose to remember who you are. Do not lose your friendship with the Scriptures, and do not stop living your life as a prayer. In war an enemy knows that, if it can neutralize communications and supply lines to food and water, everything will fall into chaos and self-destruct. Please don't let this happen to you. You are desperately needed.

Jesus explained the sobering truth of what this kind of

relationship would take. Many deserted Him because of it. In a particularly heartbreaking story found in John 6, Jesus looked at His closest friends and asked them, "Are you planning to leave too?" The apostle Peter responded to this question as we all must: "Lord, there is no one else that we can go to! Your words give eternal life" (John 6:68, CEV).

LASTLY

In conclusion I'd like to say, "Well done."

This will change everything. This broken world more than ever needs people who are awake, alert, and oriented. You are an ambassador for the kingdom of heaven, given the authority of the Almighty God with all the weight of His kingdom behind you to spread the Good News in everything you do and say. You are the physical hands and feet of Jesus, along with your brothers and sisters who make up the body of Christ. Hold your head high, knowing exactly who you are. Fight the good fight of faith, knowing that how you live your life will affect not only those who share this patch of history with you but for generations to come. You are carrying a noble banner forward out of the Scriptures and into the present. The story of God *with* us rolls on, and you play a vital role.

In the words of the great Billy Graham, "We are the

Bibles the world is reading; we are the creeds the world is needing; we are the sermons the world is heeding."

Go and live a fully reframed and nourished life with God. Orient yourself to Him through a deep friendship with the Scriptures. You are a living, breathing embarrassment to the kingdom of darkness, and the weight of your life is utterly profound to the future.

Give of yourself in ways that no one will ever be able to return.

Be brave and upright. Be without fear in the face of your enemies. Speak the truth always, even if it leads to your death. Safeguard the helpless and do no wrong. Unleash the power of mass creation by your love. Live your story inspired by God. And in all of this . . .

May the Lord bless you and keep you;

May He make His face to shine upon you and be gracious to you.

May He lift up His countenance on you and give you peace.

May the strength of God go with you;

May the wisdom of God instruct you;

May the hand of God protect you;

May the word of God direct you.

May you be sealed in Christ this day and forevermore. Amen.[3]

Notes

1. *Merriam-Webster Collegiate Dictionary, Eleventh Edition*, s.v. "inspiration."
2. Ibid.
3. See Numbers 6:24-26 and St. Patrick's Prayer for the Faithful.

IN CLOSING

Perhaps you're ready to restart your relationship with God—maybe even more than ready. May the following prayer be the beginning of that conversation.

God,

You are beautiful beyond description. I see that now. You saw me safely into this world and have pursued me every moment since. I've simply been unaware of how deep Your longing is for me. I thought this was all about my longing for You. I'm sorry about that. And I'm thankful for this chance to start something beautiful with You. Change me. I want to be made whole.

I give You access to everything. I trust You with all of it. I give You permission to touch all of the broken places in me. I give You access to my secrets. I invite You to be with me in my suffering and doubt as well as my joy. I want You to be a part of who I really am behind the personality and posing. I want You to be the most important part of my identity. So I invite You into the truest part of who I am.

Nothing is off limits to You now. No secret closets. Nothing shoved under the rug. No dark basements between us. You can go into any of those places. I trust You even there. I believe Your heart is good toward me. I trust You more than I trust anyone, and I want this relationship deeply. I love You.

I love You.

I love You.

And my heart is good toward You. I'm throwing away any gossip I've heard about You. I want to know You for myself. I want You here. With me. Always. I want to experience everything in life with You. I've been hungry for this, and I see that now. I just didn't know how badly You wanted the same thing. This changes everything. I can't imagine not experiencing life together with You. I don't want to miss another chance to make a memory with You. I want to look back in a million years and remember things we did together now, so I give myself body, soul, spirit, heart, mind, and will to You. I'm Yours and You are mine.

And there is no "Amen" as if our conversation is over. You are invited into everything I ever do and say from now on . . .

ACKNOWLEDGMENTS

With all books there are many people to thank. A book doesn't happen in a vacuum. Well, it sort of does, but getting it to the finish line doesn't happen without a team. I thank God for my team.

My thanks are first to God for letting me write this. This reframe has given me a restart with Him in ways that I hadn't even considered.

I thank my wife, Jill, who is truly an inspiration to me. Her fiery red hair and her loveliness have carried me through a life of constant transitions. Her grace and commitment have been the foundation that made it possible to navigate this work and the work of ministry.

My children: Tyler, Cristian, China, Maxwell, and baby Ezekiel remain the most profound reminder of true love in my life. Each of their personalities shows me constantly how profound and deep the love of God is for us.

My father, Rev. Ed Hardin, will always remain the man I am most indebted to, for he gave me the foundation on which I stand as a man and as a minister. Although he has passed from this life, the weight of his life is felt every day in my own.

I thank my beautiful mother. Her grace and kindness to me through all of life's seasons is a treasure. She is a picture of what it is like to be lovely.

I thank my brother Jaymey for being an encouraging inspiration to me, and his lovely wife Lindsay for being an inspiration to him.

I thank the dailyaudiobible.com community I serve for making the rhythm of the Scriptures a global family.

Thank you, Mike Greenberg, for friendship, great ideas, and stimulating conversation.

I thank Sarahjane Morronne for helping me keep life in order and travel schedules from making me crazy.

Many thanks to Jim Chaffee for good counsel and deeply appreciated honesty.

Thank you to Chris Sorensen for deep friendship, wise counsel, and a pastor's heart, and for having my back.

Many thanks to Brad Mathias for being an ally, a brother, and a friend.

Thank you to Bonnie Arends and Stephen Hadley for your loyalty to the DAB.

Thank you to Don Pape and the entire NavPress team for believing the message of *Reframe* was important. I am grateful.

Thanks to Janene MacIvor for chiseling the first draft lovingly.

The art of bringing a manuscript from draft to publication is like the relationship described in this book—discuss, question, reframe, clarify, prune, strengthen, resolve, and move forward—to the next paragraph. Thank you, Caitlyn Carlson, for the craftsmanship you brought and the life you gave to this message.

And thank you to everyone else in the world sharing this patch of history. We're in this together, and I don't want to leave anyone out.

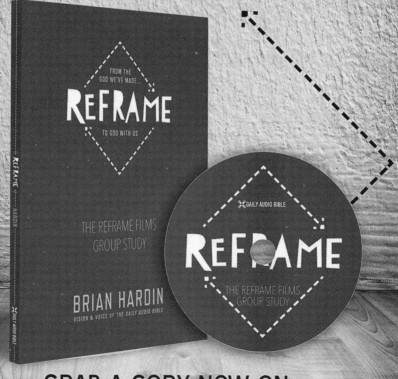

through the
BIBLE
IN A YEAR
among friends

GIVE IN TO THE **LOVE OF YOUR LIFE**

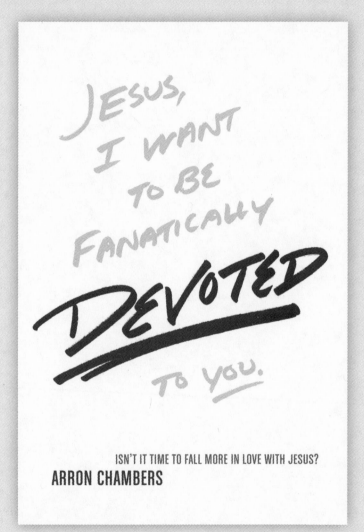

ISN'T IT TIME TO FALL MORE IN LOVE WITH JESUS?
ARRON CHAMBERS

Devoted | 978-1-61291-637-8